BULGARIA

HISTORY
RETOLD IN BRIEF

Valeria Fol, Nikolai Ovcharov
Raina Gavrilova, Borislav Gavrilov

BULGARIA

HISTORY
RETOLD IN BRIEF

Editor: Prof. Alexander Fol,
Dr. Litt., PhD

RIVA
2003

BULGARIA
HISTORY RETOLD IN BRIEF
© Assoc. Prof., PhD Valeria Fol
Assoc. Prof., PhD Nikolai Ovcharov
Assoc. Prof., PhD Raina Gavrilova
Assoc. Prof., PhD Borislav Gavrilov

© Nadia Filipova
Diana Doukovska
Roumiana Delcheva, translation

© Tim Lord, style editor
© Petroushka Tomova, editor
© Vesselin Tsakov, artist

Riva Publishing House, 2003
ISBN 954-8440-21-0

CONTENTS

I. LANDS AND PEOPLES

Varna: the starting point of Europe

The modern linguistic term *Indo-European* signifies the ancient peoples whose languages formed a family that was fundamentally different from the *Semitic*. Indo-Europeans can be identified from Europe to India from the 3rd Millennium BC onwards. One widespread concept (the migration theory) claims that originally they inhabited a region which ethnically and demographically was exclusively their own and the seed of a diaspora. The Indo-European *land of origin* continues to be sought in Northern Europe, Asia Minor, Anterior and Central Asia where a proto-language was believed to exist from which all languages evolved when the communities that spoke them settled in their historically documented habitations, and some later produced magnificent and powerful writings in Sanskrit, Iranian (Persian), Old Greek and Latin. Early migration became possible owing to the domestication of the horse which was used both for traction and riding.

Archaeological excavations in Southeastern Europe in the past 30 years have enabled another hypothesis to take hold. This hypothesis claims that both nomads and land tillers (a settled population) were involved equally in the Indo-Europeanisation process in the Carpathian, Black Sea, Aegean and Asia Minor regions.

An internationally famous site that supported this more realistic theory is the necropolis that was excavated in 1972 on the northern bank of Lake Varna. The 300 or so graves that have been brought to light so far provide evidence of a stratified and well organised society governed by aristocrats. A probable ruler stands out and can be identified by the magnificent funeral offerings and some regalia (a scepter). Dated to the latter half of the 4th Millennium BC

(Chalcolithic/Eneolithic Age), theVarna Necropolis provides sufficient data about the two still anonymous components of the coastal population.On the one hand, these
data allow a reliable recreation of the steppe nomadic military and political hierarchy of the community; on the other
hand, they illustrate the centuries-long experience in pottery, copper ore extraction, farming, marine trade, and first
and foremost, the inimitable production of gold articles
for religious and ceremonial practices.

The combination of the prehistoric skills and knowledge of the mounted people, sailors and local population
produced the *first European civilisation*, i.e. the first well-
knit and organised social entity near Varna and elsewhere
along the Western Black Sea coast. This surprising awareness is illustrated best by the differing funeral rites for poor
and rich but also by sepulchral monuments to persons
whose bodies lie elsewhere (cenotaphs) and by symbolic
graves. The clay faces in the graves decorated with gold
plates and ornaments, the so-called *masks*, suggest a very
advanced stage of abstract thinking about the divinity of
the interacting cosmic elements in the Beyond: Earth, Water and Fire (= Gold) are particularly challenging. It is only
this type of thinking and the early phase of (Indo-European) speech corresponding to it that could transform an area
with geographic features and economy into a cultural and
historical area which was socially and professionally organised to such a high extent that resolutely precludes the
obsolete theory of matriarchy.

The theory that Southeastern Europe with its Black Sea
and Asia Minor lands was the most developed centre when
Indo-European tongues and cultures took shape after the
end of the 4th Millennium BC is corroborated by the un-
broken continuity in the life of a number of settlements in
that region from the Neolithic to the Eneolithic and the
Bronze to the Iron Age. Their settlers were gradually consolidated into individual peoples which in the 1st Millen-

nium BC were finally designated with collective ethnic names in Old Greek records. The best known of these are the *Hellenes, the Thracians and the Illyrians*.These covered the southern parts of the Balkan Peninsula with the Aegean Basin and its eastern and western half to the south of the Carpathian Mountains.

The Trojan heroes

The second half of the 2nd Millennium BC starts inThrace with a remarkable accidental find at the village of Vulchitrun near the town of Pleven (Central North Bulgaria). The find is a set of large and small gold vessels, lids and a unique trichotomous receptacle whose three parts are connected by tubes to mix the holy liquids wine (blood), water, milk, olive oil and honey. These *objets d'art* that weigh 12.5 kilograms were owned by a majestic ruler. He had the power to perform religious libations with the vessels and, therefore, the functions of a high priest.

This figure is an epitome of a centralised socio-political organisation where the king was vested with judicial, military and religious power. In Southeastern Europe such an organisation is named *Mycenean* after the formidably fortified royal residence in Mycenae in the Peloponnes which was the legendary stronghold of *the king of kings* Agamemnon who, Homer says, led the Hellenic kings (basileuses) and their armies in the ten-year siege of Troy. The archaeological *Mycenean culture* from the second half of the 2nd Millennium BC is excellently documented with the *cyclopean type* of building (huge stone blocks), metal extraction and metal working, ceramics, painting and goldsmithery and also with the earliest Hellenic script (Linear B). The Vulchitrun set of gold vessels designated for rituals is the most convincing proof that ancient Thracian lands were part of the Mycenean world.

Thracian-Hellenic convergence culminated in the most dramatic event of that age, the Trojan War (13th Century BC). Troy was a city with a port on the northwestern Asia Minor coast of the Hellespont (the Dardanelles) which controlled the shipping in the straits from and to the Sea of Marmara and the Black Sea and stood in the way of Mycenean expansion to the east and northeast.

Homer extolled the heroes of the great war in the *Iliad* and in the *Odyssey*. He mentioned the Thracians in Chersonesus Thracica (Peninsula of Gallipoli) and in the lands along the northern Aegean coast from where many Trojan allies joined the war. Rhesos was the most famous of the Thracian kings. He and his suite rode to the city walls on horses that were whiter than snow and as fast as the wind; his chariot was decorated with gold and silver; his weapons were huge and made of gold. They were fit for gods, is the conclusion of that passage from Book Ten of the *Iliad*. So when Rhesos and his warriors, drooping with fatigue, fell asleep, Odysseus and Dioemedes sneaked in their camp during the night and killed them all.

The appearance of Trojan allies from Thrace is completely understandable because the Thracian ethnic and linguistic community comprised also the whole of Northwest Asia Minor with Troas. Even in Homeric antiquity these regions were part of a large zone of contact between the centres along the big rivers in Southeastern Europe: the Istros (Danube), the Axios (Vardar), the Strymon (Strouma), the Nestos (Mesta) and the Hebros (Maritza) and those in Mycenean Greece. The cultural and historical rapprochement between Thrace and Ancient Greece as a forerunner of the future Hellenisation of the southern Balkan Peninsula was the subject of poetic myths in Euripides' tragedy "Rhesos". The great tragic poet extolled the Thracian king who was turned into a demon in human form and an immortal oracle of Dionysus in the underground shrine of the god in Mount Pangaeus (on the

Aegean coast between the mouths of the Strymon and Nestos rivers).

That mercy was given in the mythical story by Athene, the goddess of wisdom. That insight of the Euripidean myth is to be attributed to the postwar historical reality as the victory of some and the defeat of others resulted in destinies that they were to share. The war weakened the rivals and caused internal redivision of territories possessed while the process was stepped up by the replacement of the bronze alloy (copper and tin) by iron as the main material from which tools, weapons and craft objects were made. Seafaring pirates pillaged kingdoms in Asia Minor and islands in the Eastern Mediterranean and extended their threat even as far as Syria, Palestine and Egypt. Meanwhile new peoples emerged in the southeast. Of these the Phryges who occupied the lands locked between the Black Sea and Mount Ida (Karadag in Turkey) were the best known. They moved from southwest Thrace where, as Herodotus testifies, originally they were called Bryges.Unlike the Thracians and the Illyrians, the Phryges in Asia Minor invented an alphabet and an early writing tradition which is reflected in the numerous inscriptions from the 6th Century BC onwards.

Thrace and the seas

After the Trojan War the Thracians sailed freely between the Pontus (the Black Sea), the Propontis (the Sea of Marmara) and the northern Aegean Sea. Records mention them as one of the peoples who exercised *thalassokratia* (marine domination) over the major sea routes. Marine supremacy enabled other Thracian communities to join the inner Mediterranean migration. At the very end of the 2nd Millennium BC Thracians from Europe seized Troas again and settled in northwest Asia Minor where their kingdom

Bithynia was to emerge later.

The population of the islands of Lemnos, Naxos, Imbros, Thassos and Samothrake was Thracian until these were Hellenised in the early 1st Millennium BC. Conditions were created in *Thracia Pontica* for ethnic, cultural, economic and religious communication among the littoral inhabitants south of Haemus (Stara Planina) to Phrygia and the isles of Greece.

The most imposing expression of similarities in that zone is the so-called megalithic culture. The large stone monuments (megaliths) were tombs and sanctuary niches, libation or sacrificial sites, shrines, stages for ritualistic processions, temples and sepulchers all cut in the rocks. The dolmens or monolithic tombstones that vary in structure and arrangement in compounds and the menhirs or votive standing stones are to be classified with these monuments. The megaliths were common in all Eurasia and in Africa in one period of pre-history or another; however, where similar ethnic and cultural circles intersected (and the Thracian, Hellenic and Phrygian did in the period in question), these functioned for one and the same religious and funeral practices which were posited on the faith in the *Earth* (*Rock*), *the Water, the Air and the Fire.*

These four underlying cosmogonic elements were deified all around; however, in the post-Trojan War period when writing was yet non-existent and in the first centuries of the 1st Millennium BC they were interrelated to the personified Great Mother Goddess (the Rock with its womb) and her Son (Heaven – Sun – Fire) whom she self-conceived immaculately and in touch with Water as a life-giving and purifying element.

The period of various *thalassokratias* ended circa 8th Century BC when control over the seas passed into the hands of the Hellenes, especially those who lived eastern-most: the inhabitants of the western Asia Minor coast who spoke an Ionian dialect and who in the 8th CenturyBC created the first *poleis* (city states). The *poleis* became parent states (metropolises) of colonies which were created along the Mediterranean European coast and even in Egypt where navigation was easy.

The creation of these cities or the Great Hellenic Colonisation (8th–6th Centuries BC) produced polis-type settlements along the Thracian banks of the river Strymon as far as the Istros. Among the cities that throughout Antiquity remained meeting places of Thracian and Hellenic culture and a scene of their mutual diffusion, the following are mentioned by ancient authors: Abdera (at the mouth of the river Nestos), Maroneia (at today's Maronia in Greece), Aenos (Enez at the mouth of the river Hebros in Thrace), Perinthos (Eregli on the northern coast of the Sea of Marmara in Turkey), Byzantion (Istanbul), Apollonia Pontica (Sozopol), Mesambria (Nessebur), Odessos (Varna), Dionysopolis (Balchik), Byzone (Kavarna), Kallatis (Mangalia in Romania), Tomis (Constanta in Romania) and Istria (at the mouth of the river Istros in Romania).

Home out of home

Such port cities emerged either where there were Thracian littoral settlements or where the coastline was most convenient and often at guarded bays that were already used by local seafarers. The colonies that the ancient Greeks called *apoikiai* (homes out of home) were not land seized after military disembarkation and campaigns against Thracian rulers in the nearby mainland. Cities emerged following a treaty between the kings and the newcomers but for one exception which is not to be doubted, Amphipolis on the Lower Strymon, conquered after a war between the Athenians and the Thracians –Edones. Epigraphs (inscriptions on stone) in Old Greek testify to such treaty-based relations which governed the division of adjacent land, with shared rights to possess and exploit it and access for Thracian royal ships to the *apoikia* ports. In partnership but also in frequent enmity the Hellenic cities along the Thracian coasts were completely integrated into the history of the vast country and continued to play a primary economic and military role in the Roman (lst–4th Centuries) and the Early Byzantine (4th–8th Centuries) age and ever after, down to the present day.

The historical viability of the coastal cities is due to the syncretism between two cultural and language elements, the Thracian and the Hellenic, from the very beginning. The diffusion of the outlooks of the illiterate Thracians and literate Hellenes created most favourable conditions for a fair coexistence of popular traditions, lifestyles, religious practices and deities in the fenced area of the *apoikiai*. There they worshipped Thracian and Hellenic but also Asia Minor and Egyptian deities; it was from there that Old Greek sprang towards the interior of the country and that Old Greek builders, painters, toreutic artists and merchants set off to the big Thracian royal cities that were away from the sea.

It was owing to the coastal cities that fast and reliable information about Thrace and the Thracians reached Old Greek travellers, adventurers, diplomats, writers and poets who, being educated, described and recreated what they had seen or heard. Their works in prose and verse *brought the Thracians into recorded history*. Their communication with Thracian culture brought that culture into the heritage of ancient Europe.

Orpheus the Thracian

The poet, singer, oracular priest, king, healer and founder of a doctrine became a character in ancient Greek literature and art from the 6th Century BC onwards. Ancient authors are unanimous that Orpheus was a poet on a par with Homer and quote (in Old Greek and in Latin) his "verses". These texts present, though in different versions, a unified concept of the creation of the Universe, the birth of gods and the behaviour and destinies of the initiated follower, i.e. systematic cosmogony, theogony, eschatology and ethics.

The Orphic doctrine, at least in the form that it has been handed down with the mediation of ancient men of letters, opposes largely the Hellenes' so-called Olympian religion which was identified in the pantheon under the aegis of Zeus and Romanised in the 3rd Century BC for the needs of Rome. The eschatological and ethical segments of the doctrine are also the most intriguing as they prescribe abstention from *breathing food* (meat), self-discipline and self-training under the instruction of a Teacher to purify the soul. After death the soul (Psyche) of an Orphic believer could transmigrate into other bodies (metempsychosis); however, its real innermost objective was to reach the underworld of Persephone and Hades to become immortal there. That was the limit of ancient Greek thinking. A mortal Hellene would not dare claim equality with the gods.

Old Greek Orphic writers, a long string starting with Onomacritus, a poet, and with Pythagoras in the 6th Century BC to Plato (4th Century BC) and extending to 6th Century writers and poets, elaborated on an oral religious doctrine, the so-called *Thracian Orphism*. That doctrine preceded Orphic philosophy and literature and existed in parallel throughout the pagan ancient times in Southeastern Europe. It does not have an ethnic attribution but indicates that among all areas where the oral religious doctrine originated and spread for long (Boeotia, Thessaly, Phocis with Delphi, East Macedonia), the islands of Samothrake, Lemnos, Naxos and Thassos in Thracia Pontica from the Strymon to the Istros, it was absorbed most thoroughly, survived till the beginning of the Christian epoch (4th Century) and was even handed down in folklore relicts.

Archaeological, literary, epigraphic, numismatic and ethnological data clearly outline the two levels of Thracian Orphism. The popular and mass aspects rested on trustful thinking, *enthusiasmos*, i.e. on the implantation of God (possession) in the believer. The aristocratic level was inspired by trustful thinking, *ekstasis*, in other words, by exaltation to god. Those who fell to enthusiasmos hoped that divine possession would purge them (rid them) of evil; those who fell to ekstasis were convinced that they would achieve complete (psycho-somatic) *immortality*. As ancient Greek observers report, they *immortalised themselves* by religious practices and sacred melodious recitation.

The two socially equal components of that oral doctrine were posited on the belief of the self-conception of the Great Mother Goddess who gave birth to her Son: however, in order to set the world in motion, she entered into *holy marriage* (incest, hierogamy) with him. Their male child is the Teacher, the oracle, the king, and the singer of the Cosmos. Because *all music is of Thracian and Asian origin*, as Old Greek literary tradition claims, and as *music is Knowledge*, *so Orpheus* extolled the two deities in their various incarnations known both in Southeastern Europe and Asia Minor.

The common folk would invoke the gods at night amid the hissing of wooden pipes (flutes), the beat of cymbals and the rhythm of kettle-drums. The figures of Cybele/Bendis/Cottyto/Hipta (Thracian and Phrygian names of the Great Mother Goddess) and of her Son who was called Zagreus or Sabazius on either side of the Bosporus and the Hellespont emerged. If the Great Mother Goddess appeared as a vision of the faith in her image of a Mountain with a cave womb, the Son most frequently assumed the hypostasis of a *bull* which during the rite was slaughtered, torn to pieces and eaten by the possessed. He was reborn in the hypostasis of a *wolf* (dog). That rebirth of the divinity was considered to be a consequence of the ritualistic holy marriage in the consummation of which the bull's blood was soaked into the Mother Earth to make her pregnant. That moment was the *ritualistic mystery* proper which participants were forbidden to relate. They were *mystai*, i.e. initiates.

When the bull died he was called in Old Greek Dionysus (= Zagreus). The Son-Fire (= Blood) was reborn and called Helios (Sun) or Apollo (= Wolf). He was also Apollonos Hyperboreos because just as the wolves came from the north (beyond the northern Thracian wind Boreas), so it came from the south. The world was divided into a dark section *Beyond* which was ruled by Dionysus and a light section *Insight* which was ruled by Helios = Apollo. So unlike the mystery of the enthusiasmos followers, the mystery of the exalted (the ecstatic) believed that they - the chosen and the initiated – were an offspring of the holy marriage from the moment when the Son-Sun touched the Great Mother Goddess with his rays.

It was the reason why Kotys I (383–359 BC), the remarkable king of the Thracians, the Odrysai in the valleys of the Hebros and the Tonzos (Toundja) called himself *a son and a servant of Apollo* in one of his inscriptions while an Orphic successor of his later called himself *a son of Helios and of the Mother Mountain.*

Aristocratic and esoteric Thracian Orphism flowed into Early Christianity and dissolved in it; however, traces of the popular Orphism can be detected by scholars and tourists even today. If anyone wants to see the Son-Fire (Dionysus) die as a sacrificial male animal, be dismembered and eaten and the believers play barefoot on embers just as 3,000 years ago, let them go to any of the villages in

Northern Greece where this rite has survived on the feast
day of SS Constantine and Helen (May 21–23). The great
Emperor and his mother replaced the old co-equal divinities Goddess Earth and her Son that Orpheus theThracian
eulogized in the Christian calendar of immovable feasts.

II. THE THRACE
OF THE PRIEST-KINGS

Said and unsaid

Unlettered (non-literary) societies are those where know-ledge of the workings of nature and of humans and of their innermost essence was kept by men who ranked first in terms of background and wealth. The teachers (priests or priest-kings) handed down the oral tradition that had been treasured by the previous generations, to the chosen ini-tiates.

It was only seldom when sacred formulae had to be in-scribed on objects dedicated to gods or invoking gods that characters were borrowed from neighbours with a script. Such Thracian inscriptions on vessels and jewels made of precious metal and on pottery, rocks, stones and tombs can be read today because the characters are Old Greek, but cannot be well understood. The language in which they are written was comprehensible only to initiated aristo-crats who would not divulge it as they were under oath; moreover, these texts were to stay with them in the grave, that gateway to the Afterlife in the Orphic religion.

It was only after centralised power was strengthened that a need arose for administrative, military and judicial regulation and for messages to be sent in diplomatic rela-tions with partners near and far. An alphabet was not in-vented and writings were not produced in Thrace because the vast country remained torn into kingdoms,independent districts and city territories which were organised on the Hellenic pattern. When the most powerful Thracian rulers needed legitimacy in writing to prove their domestic power to rivals or partners, they expressed their will and stance in Old Greek which was the lingua franca of the day.

Ancient Greek society was lettered since the *poleis* in Hellas, over 200 in number, in the 8th–5th Centuries BC formed a well-knit entity of states in a small built-up and fortified area. This necessitated spreading knowledge of the macro- and the microcosm and of what people had done and were doing and even to make it a subject of public education, the so-called *paideia*. This awareness of the importance of writing sprang up around the mid–6th Century BC when the Athenian tyrant Pisistratos ordered a team of men of letters to commit to writing Homer's two poems. Thus oral epic poetry which had been melodiously recited for many centuries for the ancient Greek basileuses or in public places for glorification and as a moral lesson became literature and a desk book in the Hellenic schools.

When old Greek prose emerged after memory of the past was strengthened as writings were added to oral tradition, so the world assumed wholeness in the minds of people. The Thracians and other major European contemporaries of the Greeks – the Celts, Scythians, Illyrians and Iberians – persisted in abstaining from writing as a means of signalling that they existed and remained *the always present Other One*, noticed in image and action.

The Thracians were the unavoidable and closest Other for the Hellenes. Along with Orpheus, poetic existence in Old Greek mythology was acquired by the singer Tamiris and the wise man Linos and Eumolpos Thrax who is the founder of mysteries in the holy town of Eleusis not far from Athens. It appears the Athenians were best informed about the Thracians as even in the 5th Century BC exquisite ceramic vessels depicted the legend of Orpheus – both his song to the Son-Sun to which armed Thracian notables lent an ear and the story of the Bacchants tearing Orpheus to pieces. That famous Greek polis made the Thracian long cloak of wool, the colourful *zeira*, fashionable and embraced the cult of the Thracian Great Mother Goddess

Bendis; it was there that Phidias sculpted Thracian horsemen on the Parthenon frieze. Herodotus and Thucydides,
the great 5th Century BC historians, described in detail the
Thracian kingdoms, lifestyle, divinities and customs in the
vast northern country for those who read and who were
read to; Plato even analysed the doctrine of immortality in
his story of the priest-king Zaimoxis who was the northern
counterpart of the Rhodopean Orpheus, the Teacher of the
Getai, theThracians who were said to be "unsurpassed in
justice and courage".

Yet what else remains hidden in the unsaid?

Dynasties

When the corpus of domestic Thracian archeological source materials is added to external records and evidence, first
it becomes clear that unlike the ancient Greek city states
Thrace was organised along *ethnic lines*. The term was
coined by Aristotle. Ethnic community-based organisation
was normal for vast areas where rural territories were ad-
ministrated by military vicegerents. These were members
of the council of *high-born men* around the ruler who controlled the centralised treasury, directly levied taxes on and
extracted gifts from his subjects, dispensed justice and
were at the head of the army. The army consisted of aristocrats who made up the heavily armed cavalry and also cav-
alrymen with lighter weapons, and infantrymen who were
forcibly recruited in the villages to be home guards.

In the latter half of the 1st Millennium BC the *ethnic
communities* created powerful kingdoms in Illyria,
Paeonia, Epirus, Thessaly and Macedonia. In Thrace they
were more numerous as to the north the country bordered
on the southern Carpathian range; to the northeast it
stretched as far as the Dniester and the Dnieper; to the west
and southwest it comprised the valley of the Strymon down

to the mouth of the Axios; to the south it included the contiguous mainland of the Hellenic Aegean *apoikiai* between the Rhodopes and the coast; and to the southeast, the landlocked Thracian sea Propontis with northwest Asia Minor.

Among the communities that were organised along ethnic lines in that incredibly motley ancient area there were five with dynastic families that deservedly became part and parcel of pre-Roman recorded history.

Writings and archaeological evidence locate the *Getai* in the lower reaches of the river Istros. Kothelas is their first ruler to have been explicitly mentioned. Philip of Macedon took his daughter Meda to be his wife when in 339 BC he formed an alliance with Kothelas against the Scythians. At least seven of Kothelas' successors are mentioned in texts and inscriptions. Dromichaetes (late 4th-early 3rd Centuries BC) was the most popular among them. He took Lisymachus, Alexander the Great's eminent general who obtained Thrace on the division of the empire of Philip's son, prisoner of war, had a feast with him and then released him. The story runs that Dromichaetes's prisoner had his food served in gold and silver plates whereas the host's food and drink was in wooden and horn bowls, the intention being to show how meaningless it was to be at war with the like of him.

The reign of Burebistas (c. 62/55–44 BC) was the heyday of the Getan dynasty when this contemporary of Gaius Julius Caesar strengthened his rule from the Carpathian Mountains to the Black Sea south of Haemus.The Getai were already called Dakoi, first in Latin and then in Old Greek sources and by that popular name stayed in the front stage of military and political history over the last decades of the 1st Century till AD 107, when the Roman Emperor Trajan (AD 98–117) after the bloodbath of two wars, conquered the kingdom of their heroic King Decebalus. The victory was commemorated at the Forum Trajanum in the centre of which the famous column was placed with depictions of the Dacian Wars.

The Thrace of the *Triballi* stretched west of the river Oxios (Iskur), in what is today Northwestern Bulgaria and Northeastern Serbia. They were wide known for their horrifying army which often made incursions down to the Aegean Sea to plunder villages and lands. The Athenian comic poet Aristophanes likened it to a swarm of locusts. Except for Syrmos, an enemy whom Alexander the Great defeated on the battlefield, none of their rulers is mentioned explicitly and with certainty. Led by Syrmos, the Triballi retreated in legitimate battle north of Haemus when Alexander who had just become king moved fast to the Istros in order to secure his rear before the campaigns against the empire of the Persians in the east began.

The *Bessi* inhabited the lands south of Haemus in the Rhodope Mountains and in some valleys on the way to the foothills. Their ethnic-based military and political organisation was stable even in the 5th Century BC from when the earliest facts date about the mountain shrine of the principal Orphic god who was the Son of the Great Mother Goddess and who authors most often called Dionysus. Randomly mentioned names of kings seem to allow attribution to that dynasty, yet Vologaeses, a priest (and king?) in the shrine who led one of the most sweeping Thracian uprisings against the Romans invading the peninsula in late 1st Century BC is the most credible name.

The *Edones* who are known from Homer's epic with their King Rhesos controlled southwest Thrace in the lower reaches of the Strymon with a centre, Mount Pangaeus, which was rich in gold deposits. There are only two reliably recorded names of kings of the Edones in sources and on coins from the late 6th Century BC to the conquest of their state by Philip II in the 50s of the 4th Century BC. To compensate for this scarcity, impressive facts are reported about their abilities as warriors in battles won in the 5th

Century BC against none less than the Athenians who lost many lives before they seized the key Edonian centre, the Nine Ways, on the Strymon, where they founded Amphipolis.

The ethnonym Odrysai refers to all Thracians from the upper reaches of the Tonzos (Toundja) to the mouth of the Hebros together with the lands around and parts of the Rhodopes, Sakar and Strandja mountains and also to the Thracians from the mainland of Old Greek colonies along the Aegean Sea, the Sea of Marmara and the Black Sea. The Odrysian state first came to the attention of Hellenic writers with the actions of Teres (c. 490–464 BC).

The first ruler of the Odrysai very cleverly took advantage of the campaign of Darius I across Eastern Thrace, Haemus and the Istros against the Scythians. The Persian Empire of the Achaemenid dynasty that was the major power in Euro-Asia started its expansion in 514/512 BC seeking to subdue the whole Black Sea basin; however, Darius was unable to defeat the mounted Scythian army in the bare Pontic steppe. When the king of kings withdrew from north to south where his point of departure was in the area of Propontis and the Straits, Teres took advantage of the military and political vacuum that was formed and in the 80s of the 5th Century went as far as the lower reaches of the Istros, made it the northern border of his kingdom and concluded a treaty of alliance with the Scythian rulers.

Although the Scythian campaign was a failure it is believed that Darius thereby created a bridgehead on the continent by organising a European (Aegean) *satrapy*, i.e. a military administrative district. Despite the Persian presence with garrisons left there to maintain it, Teres, and it is no wonder that Thucydides wrote he was the real founder of the kingdom of the Odrysai, penetrated deep into the southeast as far as Byzantion where he set his new border.

The sons of Teres, Sparadokos (c. 464–444 BC) and Sitalkes (c. 444–424 BC), were mentioned first after the mid 5th Century BC. These two made the kingdom of the Odrysai the largest ethnic-based state in the Balkan Peninsula. Thucydides describes it as a triangle whose base is the imaginary line from the mouth of the Nestos in the Aegean Sea to the mouth of the Istros in the Black Sea. The First Athenian Maritime Alliance became the real enemy of the Odrysai after the Greco-Persian Wars and the peace treaty of 464. Athens gradually evolved as a sea power after the Persians were defeated and the Greek *poleis* in Asia Minor were liberated by a large fleet, military settlers in the eastern Aegean islands and also by annual tribute levied on the allies. The first convincing evidence of the might of the Odrysian dynasty was provided by the proven sharing between the dynasty and Athens of this tribute which was paid by the cities on the Aegean and the Marmara coast. In addition to the money, the treasury of the Odrysai acquired as gifts precious metals and luxury articles which the Odrysian kings demanded from embassies, allies and the vanquished. The highest figure reported about the Odrysian treasury is 1000 talanta (= 250 tons in metal/coins) which seems indicative of the reign of Sitalkes' successor Seuthes I (424–407/405BC). The Odrysian royal residence and treasury that contemporaries locate in Hieron Oros (The Holy Mount), today's Tekirdag in European Turkey, is about to be excavated.

The conflict with the Athenian Maritime Alliance was also provoked by military pressure on the part of the Odrysai. Sitalkes took advantage of the Peloponnesian War between this Alliance and the Peloponnesian League with Sparta at the head (431–404 BC) and tried with a 150,000 strong army to conquer Eastern Macedonia and the peninsula of Chalcidice on both sides of the bay of Thessaloniki. He could not hold out against the enemy but after his death on the battlefield against the Triballi in the northwestern corner of the kingdom of the Odrysai, Seuthes I found a more promising direction for expansion and sought to conquer Chersonesus Thracica and thus assume control over the maritime routes that were vitally important for Athens as these supplied the city with grain and enabled it to trade. Seuthes did not complete his successful military operations.

Kotys I (383–359 BC) who was probably his son was an energetic general, a hypocritical diplomat and a cruel ruler; he was killed by Athenian mercenaries in one of his residences on the coast in the year when Philip II assumed the title of King of Macedon. The murder put an end to hypocritical diplomacy and to the merciless war between Athens, which defended possessions in Chersonesus Thracica in order to retain control over the maritime routes, and Kotys, whose plans were more ambitious than his kingdom could afford. The king of the Odrysai subdued the northern Aegean coast which he put under military and financial control and conquered the strategic peninsula and virtually all its cities. However, he overestimated his actual capacity and underestimated the still solid reserves of Athens, though he was the first in Southeastern Europe to foresee how hegemony would soon be established by force over the city states in Hellas so as to unite them under one-man rule. Indeed this was going to be the outcome of the economic and political crisis in Hellas but history had decreed that the leading role was to be played by other actors who were born somewhat later when all Old Greek *poleis* were in total impasse due to poverty and impotence. These actors were the Macedonian Hellenes, Philip II and his son Alexander, surnamed the Great.

Philip II of Macedon sought to expand to the east towards and beyond the Strymon with an army which was the best of the day. Kotys was dead and Odrysian Thrace was divided in three. After conquests in the south Philip eliminated two of the Thracian kings and in the 40s of the 4th Century BC he seized the core of the Odrysian kingdom ruled by the son of Kotys, Kersebleptes (359–341 BC). The Macedonian army advanced along the valley of the Hebros-Tonzos as far as Cabile (at today's Yambol), and to the city of the seven mounts called Philippopolis (Poulpoudeva in Thracian and Plovdiv in Bulgarian).

However the Macedonian rule in Thrace was in the form of the presence of two or three garrisons. The Odrysai survived even Alexander the Great's campaign to and across the Danube. Seuthes, surnamed the Third, probably a son of Kotys I (c.330–302/301 or 297 BC) fought and won independence from the Macedonian vicegerents in Thrace and its official rulers both during the reign of Alexander the Great and after his death in 323 BC. Thus the Odrysian statehood survived till the beginning of the Celtic invasion in 280–279 BC and many centuries after till AD 45 when Roemetalkes III, the last king who was a vassal to Rome, was killed and the Emperor Claudius (AD 41–54) made Thrace a Roman province.

The holy marriage

These Thracian kings and other dynastic families in European and in Asia Minor Thrace were statesmen, generals, judges and administrators but not only that. Old Greek and Latin records suggest and archaeological finds prove their sacral function.

First of all it has to be recalled that the ethnically-based Thracian states derived their names from the rulers' family names. Getai (Dakoi), Triballi, Bessi, Edones and Odrysai were surnames deriving from the position of a family in the religion; these were the nicknames of the families of priests who for many generations maintained and performed *the principal rite*. Although the etymology of the dynastic families and the ethnic names that derived from them is not always indisputable, they all were related to the holiest state ritualism.

The Getai believed in their Zalmoxis who persuaded them he was immortal when he spent *four years* in the cave womb and re-emerged in the *fifth year*. The Immortal Getai sent an envoy to their deified Teacher by throwing him on the blades of three spears: if the man was righteous (purged in ekstasis), he died.

The Bessi, who are explicitly reported as a family of priests, performed their rites in the Rhodopean shrine. It was a rotund structure with a gaping roof and an altar in the middle under it. In daylight when the Son-Sun(= Apollo) was in his zenith, his rays played on the altar; at night when the Sun-Fire (= Dionysus) was in the dark hemisphere of the Cosmos, flames burned on that place and sought to reach the black firmament which was strewn with stars. Priests decoded the will of their dual god both by the Sun's rays and the Fire's flames.

The Edones deified their Pangaion, i.e. the All-Earth, as the Great Mother Goddess in whose holy underground womb the deified king Rhesos interpreted what the chthonic Sun-Fire, i.e. Dionysus, had suggested to him. During the mystery celebration of the god in the Mountain, a plant cythara grew which fed on the blood of Orpheus and repeated the music of his instrument.

The Odrysai erected shrines to the Great Mother Goddess, as their family nickname suggests, in a holy oak-tree grove. If the holy grove was not capped by a rock and lay green in a valley, then they placed a piece of rock among the trees to see the image of the Great Mother Goddess and of her Son-Sun. This explains why after the 5th Century BC the Odrysian king-priest built his fortified cities around such holy places. Barracks, stables, storage premises and weapon forgeries and also the palace with the shrine were inside the walls of *the royal cities* (so-called tyrsis, i.e. towers). In the 4th Century BC the Odrysian King Seuthes III built his capital Seuthopolis (near the town of Kazanluk in Central South Bulgaria) after the Hellenic plan where the shrine with a central altar was in the king's apartments.

Productive archaeological excavations in recent years in the valley of the upper reaches of the Tonzos west of Kazanluk have produced a dozen Thracian tumuli which are impressive in size (as high as 20 meters). These rank among the best examples of such monuments which are some 19,000 in number south of the Danube alone. These mounds over a relatively small area invited the designation the Valley of Thracian (Odrysian) Kings and constituted a core of religious life at the foothills of Haemus between c. 5th and c. 2nd/lst Centuries BC, before and after Seuthes III.

Studies have proved with explicit facts the old hypothesis that the mound was not earth piled but rather ritualistically layered in keeping with the offices performed on clay sites and sacred pits where animals were sacrificed and offerings and gifts made. Therefore the mound was deliberately modelled. The model is stereometric and contains the four horizontal directions of the Cosmos in the circle at the base and the three levels of its vertical axis up to the apex of the mound. It was there that structures were first recognized which had been built under the earthwork in tunnels (niches). This building pattern demonstrates the idea that human deeds are sheltered in the divine cosmic structure and also dates it back as a tradition from *Mycenean Thrace*, i.e. as centuries-old continuity (second half of the 2nd–lst Millennium BC) in professing oral Orphic faith.

Rich dynastic tombs among the buildings exposed have been explored; some of them have geometric and floral decorations. Other cupola structures had evidently a more intricate function analysed as a mausoleum, i.e. a tomb for pilgrimage and also as a heroon, i.e. a symbolic burial of a deceased man-demon. He could be an Odrysian king-priest who was doctrinally immortalised.The compound of six premises in Ostrousha mound was built for such a function; the central premise was shaped as a sarcophagus cut in a monolith with a high stone bed, with no traces of a funeral and with a painted cellular ceiling. Regrettably the frescoes have been badly damaged.The compound over which earth had been ritualistically spread was for a long time part of the temenos (the holy area) where a, to us unknown, son of the Sun, i.e. a dead Odrysian king-priest, was worshipped.

What was the main ritual like? Once a year the king became the sole priest and performed the ritual on a rocky peak, in a holy grove or in a specially built hall which was a circle in the Thracian tradition and a rectangle in the Hellenic borrowing. There he slaughtered a horse, the sacrificial regal animal which in all Indo-European peoples completely substituted for man. The horse, the solar animal, was slaughtered and died; that is, the king-priest made a self sacrifice in order to enter through his blood flowing into the earth into a holy doctrine-sanctioned marriage with the Great Mother Goddess as a son of her Son and to give to his kingdom a new annual cycle of existence.

Rich Thracian necropolises often contain sacrificed horses and buried dogs (= wolves). In other words the *rite Beyond* covered the doctrinal Orphic existence both of the God-Sun who was reborn and of his son-priest. For the Odrysai the Son was Helios, the Orphic Hyperborean Apollo. As early as the 5th Century AD Herodotus called the initiated *happily demonic*, i.e. immortalised in their death. A small vault has been excavated in a mound in the Valley of Kings with white painted walls, with horses sacrificed at the entrance and a deliberately shaped rectangular altar. A carefully made groove led the blood into the Mother Earth. After the worship the tomb was emptied and converted into a heroon or a home of the man-demon. The white colour of the Beyond is the colour of the son of the Great Mother Goddess in whose shrine his own son is translated in a doctrinally conceived holy marriage.

Holy marriage was even depicted once by a Thracian toreutic artist who made the applique decoration for the horse trappings which were symbolically buried in a bronze vessel with its mouth stuck into the ground. The treasure was discovered during a random operation near the village of Letnitsa (Central North Bulgaria) and was buried in order to recreate the union of the king-priest, perceived as a solar animal, with the Great Mother Goddess while the silver gilded applique features the whole oral Orphic doctrine from the self-conception of the goddess to the naturalistically depicted copulation of the son of the Son with her.

When once Kotys I shouted, as the anecdote tells us, that he wanted Athene in his bed and in his desperately drunken state sent his servants to bring the goddess, he, the "priest and son of Apollo" was not pronouncing a blasphemy. His doctrinal position allowed him to wish such copulation. By the way, the Athenians had every reason to hate him.

Tetrad

The arrangement of the Letnitsa appliqued ornaments can be numerically expressed. Other Thracian monuments though, the most convincing example of which is the royal tomb in the Getan area at what is today the village of Sveshtari near the town of Isperih (Northeast Bulgaria), have an even clearer numeric pattern.

Two things are immediately noticed on entering the rectangular brickwork burial chamber with a semicylindrical roof nestling under a high layer of ritualistically piled earth on the mound. The first are the ten caryatids each with an individual face and traces of various paints on their robes. There are three figures on each of the two long walls and four stand on the shorter frontal wall. The other is the unfinished painting over the four female statues which depicts the Great Mother Goddess in a sublime moment for the king-priest when she crowns him with a crown of gold of the type which is common even in royal funerals or, in other words, she immortalises him doctrinally.

4 + 3 + 3 is a formula devised by Pythagoras after he learned and assimilated the fundamental principles of oral Thracian Orphism. The tetrad (the figure 4) is a key figure as it encodes the first four phases of the creation of the Orphic Cosmos: the Great Mother Goddess in a state of *rest*; there follow *the self-conception, the fetus, then its maturing and fourth, its birth*. Then her Son steps in triumphantly in *the fifth phase*, sets the Cosmos in motion in *the sixth phase*, and performs hierogamy in *the seventh phase*. According to Pythagoras this is the first triad. A vaulted building with white painted walls has been discovered under a mound in the Valley of the Kings. A white column with cannelures which reaches the centre of a solar rosette on the dome at a height exceeding four metres stands up in the centre of the circular stone altar. The plinth which is almost one metre high is divided by fake black columns into seven planes. This plan recreates both the axis of the Dionysian-Apollonian shrine of the Bessi and the presence of the Son in hierogamy which is emphasised by the white colour of Death and of Light.

The second triad includes the birth of the son of the Son (*the eighth phase*), his reign, i.e. the organisation of society (*the ninth phase*), and his doctrinal immortalisation (*the tenth phase*). The terrestrial and the celestial Cosmos has been created and in order to recreate itself, the faith gives meaning to the new holy marriage of the son of the Son.

The tetrad has been documented as a sacred number in ethnic divisions of areas in Thessaly and in Thrace. It has been identified in the four-plus-three-string *lyre of Orpheus* in the ascending coded order of the tones D (= Earth) – E (= Water) – F (= Air) – G (= Fire), that is, by sounding the basic cosmic elements and also in A (= the ascent of the Son) – B (= setting the world in motion) and C (= holy marriage).

However the tetrad is also well observed in the oral medium, outside the numeric-tonal equivalents of Pythagoras. The tetrad is manifested divinity for the Thracian megalithic shrine on the island of Samothrake. The Hellenisation of the shrine was completed after the 6th–5th Centuries BC; however its priests continued to officiate in their mysterious (Thracian) language till the Christian church closed it down in the 4th Century. The divine tetrad was identified in inland European Thrace by Herodotus who was the best authority on it. On Samothrake it was called by local names whereas in Thrace it was through the agency of Old Greek gods that it was perceived and understood by those for whom the "father of history" was writing.

In each of these two places *Hermes* was the god by whom the initiated swore. As Herodotus explicitly reports, the Thracian kings swore by him separately from their subjects as they considered him their forefather. An oath by a theonym is a perfect code of the *itiphallic* (fertilising) but *abstract male principle*, i.e. of the self-conception of the Great Mother Goddess resulting in the birth of the Son and of his son, the king-priest. Herodotus unmistakably identified the Thracian Great Mother Goddess as the Greek Artemis as she is a virgin and mistress of all wild nature, her son as Dionysus (= Son–Fire–Bull) and the deified king-priest as Ares the warrior. These three divinities were universally worshipped. Their corresponding theonyms on Samothrake were Axiokersa, Axieros and Axiokersos, all of them undoubtedly deriving from the idea of black (underground) Water, that is, from the self-conceiving womb of the Great Mother Goddess. When the mystai (the initiated) on Samothrake pronounced an oath, the oath was Orphic, the authors report. In other words, it was similar to that of the king-priests, the doctrinal sons of the Son.

III. FROM CRISIS TO TOLERANCE

Promise unfulfilled

When Kotys I was killed by Athenian mercenaries and Philip of Macedon ascended the Macedonian throne, both of which happened in 359 BC, changes in the historical realities in Southeastern Europe did not cease. On the contrary, these became more tangible for contemporaries in Thrace, Macedonia and Hellas. When in 336 BC Philip II was killed in a palace coup and his son Alexander immediately succeeded him, the changes occurred with the speed of whirlwind. They formed a historically promising tendency which emerged in the first half of the 4th Century BC in Odrysian Thrace and was brought to fruition by the Macedon dynasty, namely, the old Hellenic polis organisation, which, broken apart as a result of economic crises and fratricidal wars, gave way to powerful ethnic-based monarchies.

Alexander the Great did what was historically required during his short dazzling life before he died in 323 BC in Babylon. For the first time people felt *cosmopolitan*, i.e. citizens of a newly established community where all familiar forms of ownership, real estate, market relations and cultural traditions coexisted. Three centuries after the death of the inimitable conqueror and statesman that *syncretism* preconditioned the appearance of a future European community which started with the establishment of a single culture and spirituality, today known and interpreted as the *Hellenistic heritage*. It was the product of the dissemination of the Hellenistic ideas, skills and knowledge and their creative contact with those of Egypt, Asia Minor, the Semites and Iran.

The following finds rank among the unanimously acknowledged examples of syncretic Hellenistic art in

Thrace: the gold set with ritual functions from Panagyur-ishte (in the Sredna Gora Mountains, South Bulgaria), and the Kazanluk Tomb. The goldsmith who most probably came from Asia Minor used a magnificently exquisite tech-nique to depict Hellenic scenes and Hellenic-Eastern mo-tifs on the vessels. The remarkable painter of Seuthes III resorted to Hellenic-style techniques and conventional scenes to depict on the dome of the tomb the protection extended by the Great Mother Goddess to her doctrinal son/king/priest.

When in 31 BC the future first Roman Emperor Oc-tavian defeated his rival Mark Antony near Actium in Epirus, the latter being the hired admiral of the fleet of Cleopatra VII, the last Egyptian Hellenistic Queen, the southeast of Europe and the whole Afro-Asian world of Alexander the Great fell under Roman domination. The Hellenistic processes of two-way diffusion were not halted though. At least literature and the arts provided favourable conditions for exchanges of inspiration coming from all lands of the Roman Empire.

However, two developments in Hellas, Macedonia and Thrace predetermined their destinies in the Hellenistic community. The free citizens in the Greek *poleis* in the whole southeast were transformed into subjects and sub-jects were unable to take advantage of the right to settle where they wished, i.e. to be cosmopolitans, because of their quick impoverishment and involvement in endless wars.

Alexander the Great was recognized as the *hegemon* (leader) of all the Greeks on account of Philip's commit-ment which was passed onto him, to pull Hellas out of the crisis and chaos of the 4th Century BC. He did not stick to that commitment due to his utter dedication to building his world empire. The decline of Hellas continued, reached Macedonia and Thrace, and was speeded up by the Celts and the Romans.

The Celtic invasion which started from Central Europe climaxed in the southeast in the early 3rd Century BC. The invading troops who moved along with their families and chattels pillaged regions in the peninsula and particularly in Hellas. Some of the invaders crossed over to Northwest Asia Minor where they settled.

Celtic groups organised their kingdom in Thrace. It remained in existence till the 20s of the 3rd Century BC when the Thracians abolished it but their victory coincided with the beginning of the Roman conquest. This conquest started exactly in the 20s of the 3rd Century BC from the Balkan Peninsula's Adriatic coast from where the legions put down the resistance of Illyrians and reached Epirus in two successive wars.

Even while the famous Carthaginian Hannibal was waging a life-and-death war with Rome in Italy, the City provoked Macedonia, its next enemy in the East. In three wars the Roman generals destroyed the old Macedonian state and made it a province with four districts (148 BC); meanwhile they captured and destroyed Carthage in North Africa.

The Roman strategic plan envisaged the conquest of the Black Sea basin. This presupposed regular campaigns against the Thracian kingdoms. Military operations started in the late 2nd Century BC and continued for two and a half centuries. For a long time it was difficult to penetrate from the direction of the sea because of the strong coalition of Mithridates VI who was the ruler of the Pontic lands. Thracian mercenary units placed themselves under his command as early as the 80s of the 1st Century BC. One of the unit commanders was Spartacus who was to become the famous leader of the slave revolt. He was an Odrysian aristocrat who was taken prisoner of war by the Romans and forced to fight as a gladiator. Between 74 and 71 BC Spartacus subjected Italy to a devastating war, leading slaves of different backgrounds.

Rome again demonstrated its capacity to operate on several fronts and while the legions were defeating the rebels, Marcus Terentius Varro Luculus penetrated from south to north along the western Black Sea coast and conquered the Old Greek *apoikiai* and their environs.

In 29–28 BC Marcus Licinius Crassus, the grandson of the Crassus who had defeated Spartacus, conquered the Danubian Plain and the province of Moesia was instituted in 15 BC. Originally it was locked between where the Sava flows into the Danube at today's Belgrade, the Black Sea, the Danube Delta and the Balkan Range. When 30 years later the last vassal Thracian king was killed and Thrace south of Haemus was organised as a province, it was only the memory of the Thracians' courage and valour in hopeless battles that remained recorded by the Roman historian Tacitus.

Civilitas means tolerance

The Romans immediately started to organise the lands that they had conquered but were intelligent enough not to touch the community organisation of the villages which ensured normal farming, and not to expropriate the Thracian aristocrats' land holdings. Economically independent and with extensive political and administrative powers in their roles as strategists, inherited from the Hellenistic statehood and district governors, these local notables retained their status throughout the 1st Century till the early 2nd Century. The Roman provincial authorities needed them both south and north of Haemus at least as long as they gained full control of all Thracian lands. The Emperor Domitian (AD 81–96) fortified the limes (the border) in the north after the unsuccessful war with the Dakoi (Getai) by the division of Moesia into Superior and Inferior (to the west and east of the Danube's tributary, the

Tsibritsa) and in AD 107 the Emperor Trajan established a new Thracian province, Dacia after the death of his famed enemy Decebalus and moved the Empire's border to the Carpathian Mountains and Transylvania.

It was the beginning of an almost 130-year long period of rule by the houses of the Antonini and Severi during which Dacia, the two Moesias and Thrace became some of the most attractive lands in the Empire. Old villages were transformed into towns and new ones were established. Even people from as far as Asia Minor, Syria and Judaea flocked to Serdica (Sofia), Augusta Trajana (Stara Zagora) and Philippopolis (Plovdiv). Excellent roads connected all populated areas, forts and garrison camps. Some of these were laid over old tracks but also Roman engineers built many new roads in order to have a dense network with stations where horses were changed and travellers stopped to have a rest. This infrastructure was designed mainly for fast courier service and army movements from Italy and from Central Europe via the southeast to Asia Minor and vice versa. The infrastructure covered the Danubian Way, the Diagonal (to Byzantion) and the so-called Via Egnatia (along the Aegean coast) which were intersected by roads tracing the Aegean Sea-Danube-Carpathian Mountains axis.

The large-scale Roman civil works and urbanisation primarily introduced the imperial city lifestyle to all Thracian lands. It was the imperial standards which shaped the characteristics of the first all-European civilisation. That civilisation was the deed of the Roman armies and was further spread and maintained by its legions, support troops and veterans who settled in their native places or in new places. Along with Latin, which was the language of the military and civilian authorities, the provinces adopted the Roman rules of public conduct and fundamental norms of law and the habit of living in accordance with them. The armies brought in the new deities of the different peoples as the authorities allowed everyone, even the soldier, to profess his religion providing he respected the official Roman pantheon and, first and foremost, the cult of the deified emperor. As a matter of fact the persecution of Christians which was fiercest under Diocletian (AD 284–305) was provoked by the rejection of this cult and naturally by the men's objection to serving in the army.

The tolerant attitude towards the cultural and historical heritage of each people which was crucial for the existence of the Empire was deliberately fostered by the imperial administration and by the army. Even when the economic crisis and incursions of the Germans (Goths) in the 3rd Century brought back the days of internecine strife, the Empire had the power to re-establish its faithful policy during the reign of Constantine (AD 306–337) who deservedly was to be surnamed the Great.

The Horseman and Christianity

The aristocratic Orphic doctrine gradually lost its mysterious, esoteric (initiate) nature under the powerful impact of Hellenistic religious syncretism in which myths, cults and rites dedicated to gods from various religions were brought in unity and were not discriminated against. As the power of kings in Thrace weakened, their teaching was further profaned and during the Roman invasion was debased to a commonly professed faith in which social and doctrinal differences vanished. This was the worship of the Horseman.

The Horseman was modelled on votive relief tablets (placed in shrines) and for burial (placed in graves as wished by the deceased and his family) between the 1st and 3rd Century AD. Excavations and finds have produced almost 4000 such tablets. Such tablets, which are daily acquired by museums and collections, feature the Horseman in a hunting scene, often with deities, and with his name inscribed. Most common is the old Greek name *Heros*, i.e. a hero patron in the shape of a man-demon with an immortal soul, and inscriptions on the relief tablets containing religious and even rustic epithets and general definitions like *master/ruler*.

The Horseman-Hunter is the personified reliance on the omnipresence of the old principal Orphic god, the Son of the Great Mother Goddess. When his worship was profaned and the mysterious nature of the holy marriage was violated, the Horseman began to ride all over Thrace as an open exponent of the key constituents of faith: the solar animal whose galloping incarnated the life-giving movement of Helios-Apollo and which raced between the Worlds; hunting as a value characteristic of the king-priest but also as a code of the chthonic (earthly) life-giving force of the Great Mother Goddess, the mistress of Nature; and the snake. In the outgoing oral Orphism it was treated as an incarnation of the Son-Fire, i.e. of Dionysus.

These reliefs and other similar monuments with anonymous but explicitly sculpted figures of the Great Mother Goddess, of her Son who has taken the shape of a bull or a wolf, and of priests/priestesses of the mystery cults provide, together with the funeral rites that were preserved between the 1st and 3rd Century, abundant documentation of steady paganism. Its vitality is supported by written information about the reluctance of the *savage Thracians* to adopt the new religion. Yet they adopted it quite early, were lavishly praised for their humility and even became famous for two translations of the Bible. One was made in their lands by bishop Wulfila (AD 311–383) in Gothic when he was a missionary among the Eastern Goths who for some time lived in Moesia at Nikopolis ad Istrum (today's village of Nikyup, near Veliko Turnovo in Central North Bulgaria); the other was called Biblia Bessica, named after the most devout followers of Dionysus in the Rhodopes in order to emphasise how the Thracian "barbarian" tongue preached the Word of God.

Indeed the Thracians were a fertile soil for literate Christianity because their old oral Orphism tended strongly towards monotheism which was personified in the Son of the Great Mother Goddess. Pagan monotheism was even supported by arguments by some neo-Platonic writers till the 5th Century who gave as an example the Sun which they considered consubstantial and indivisible because in its two hypostases, that of Apollo and Dionysus, it embraced the whole Cosmos. Early Empire depictions present Orpheus not just in his familiar Christian metamorphosis of "God's shepherd", put by men of letters, sculptors and painters on a par with those of Abraham and Moses, but also feature him on the cross. The crucified *Orpheos Bacchicos* in the posture of suffering Christ is the closest approximation between the Orphic faith and early Christianity which seems to have started in the days of St. Paul the Apostle. The man who made Judeo-Christianity a world religion comprehensible to all preached along the Aegean coast (Thessalonica, Philippi at today's Kavalla) and his sermons penetrated Thrace to the north, even in the early years after it became a Roman province.

That is why the Horseman, the image of millennial faith hidden under a conventional Hellenistic and Roman iconography, adapted to Christianity in a most natural way. He was called St. George by worshippers whose oral tradition folklorically transformed the martyr of the church from Asia Minor into an immortal spiritual leader. In Thracian lands even the icon of St. George transfixing the dragon and the tablet with the relief of the Horseman-Hunter were and are interchangeable in the cult, something which persists to this very day. The Roman emperor who was the first to believe in them cleared the way to enlightenment.

Enlightened emperor

Flavius Valerius Constantine was born in Naissos (Nis), the son of Constantine Chlorus and Helena, in AD 272(?).Trained for a military and political career during the reign of Diocletian, he laid claim to the Empire after his predecessor's abdication. In AD 312 he won a triumphant victory over the Germani and right after that became engaged in a confrontation with his rivals Maximinus and Maxentius near Rome. Before the battle Constantine saw a cross with an inscription on it: *In hoc signo vinces* (In that sign you shall conquer) and issued an order to unfurl flags with crosses embroidered on them. The story runs that God himself helped the man who saw, read and believed. In the following year, AD 313, Constantine issued his famous edict in Mediolanum (Milan), by which he put an end to the persecution of Christians, put Christianity on a par with the remaining religions and paved the way for its ultimate adoption.

Constantine's statesmanship inspired him to move his capital to the east where the Empire's rich provinces lay. Hesitating between his native Naissos and Serdica, the Emperor chose old Byzantion, which was the choice of a genius. That city, which was founded by Doric (Megarian) colonists in the 7th Century BC, was on the site of an old Thracian settlement. It was called Byzas which was typical of Pontic Thrace, and the name survives in today's Vize/Urdoviza and suchlike. The toponym was incorporated in the myth of the city's foundation as the name of the king of the Thracians. In Byzantion they worshipped the man-demon Rhesos; vestiges of the old Thracian beliefs can be traced in the story of the snakes which accompanied the Great Mother Goddess and which women in the city threw against invaders when the men were away fighting in a war.

Constantinople, which was proclaimed a capital in AD

330, was situated in a Thracian and Hellenic environment where Rome could not prevail. The city developed its advantage to be the centre of a multiple ethnic and cultural entity which already possessed the vitality of early Christian culture. Constantinople and its territory, which lay astride two continents, formed the core of future Byzantium which was to survive by one thousand years the devastation of Rome by the Germanic tribes in the 5th Century. Meanwhile the most prominent pagan Thraco-Hellenic traces in the traditional popular culture of Southeastern Europe were preserved over that territory.

It appears that Constantine was great not only by what he did but also by what he foresaw. It was his outstanding intellect which was behind the First Ecumenical Council in Nicaea in AD 325 which formulated the Symbol of the Christian Creed. By that document the Emperor enforced the non-discrimination of tongues in the early interpretations and disputes and cleared the way for the *Chora (the territory) of Constantinople* in Southeastern Europe and in Asia Minor to become the seat of the Orthodox faith.

The foundation laid by Constantine the Great was so solid that *the barbarian invasions* did not break down the Empire's integrity. Hard times set in for the Empire around AD 275 when the Emperor Aurelian was forced to abandon Dacia. In AD 378 the Goths defeated the Emperor Valens at Hadrianople (Edirne in Turkey) and settled in Moesia. After the official division of the Roman Empire in AD 395 *the Hunnic incursions* (AD 408–467) were a sign of looming defeat. The first Bulgar mercenary detachments in the Byzantine army were formed in AD 479; the large-scale Slav settlement started at the end of that century. In the 6th–7th Centuries these waves changed the peninsula's ethnic and demographic picture south of the Carpathian Mountains down to the Aegean islands and Peloponnes; however, the Hellenic element held its own through, and in, Byzantium.

Records tell that the incursions of Goths, Huns, Avars, Bulgars and Slavs were so devastating that they left no stone unturned across the Empire. That exaggeration is to be attributed to the moral pathos of the early church writers who extolled the benevolence of God that gave to the Orthodox believers atonement for sins only through suffering.

That apocalyptic picture in records summarised in the phrase *Attila the Scourge of God* is not corroborated by archaeological, epigraphic, linguistic and ethnographic sources. These indicate that virtually all cities in Southeastern Europe experienced the turbulence whereas villages in highlands and mountains were not plundered. Naturally the ethnic and demographic composition in Southeastern Europe changed as new population groups emerged. Some of them settled forcibly and as conquerors even exacted a tax from the population around; others were labelled by Constantinople *foederati* (allies) in order to be opposed to newly coming invaders.

It is hardly possible to establish the proportion of the indigenous Thracian population to the new settlers, the "barbarians" of Germanic, Slav and Turkic origin, who spoke their respective languages. Such a proportion is impossible to establish concerning the population in cities which were a melting pot despite Romanisation to the north and Hellenisation to the south of Haemus. In some mountains though, the Rhodopes for example, the Thracian population was not assimilated till the 10th–11th Centuries.

Most recent studies have shed light on another line of continuity between Antiquity and the Middle Ages. They rest on the extraction and family background of some of the first early Byzantine emperors after Constantine the Great, and draw attention to the evident possibility for this to be the reason for elements of the old Thracian religion preserved in rites and in imperial protocol to have been Christianised and adopted. The list understandably excludes the emperors installed by garrisons, armies and armed coups (the so-called soldier-emperors) during the 3rd Century crisis such as Maximinus Thrax (AD 235–238).

Marcianus, a soldier and the son of a soldier, was born in Thrace and was Byzantium's Emperor for a relatively short time (AD 450–457); Leo I (AD 457–474) had a long reign and a pious one, as recorded. He was Thracian but also known as Bess which in the 5th Century no more made any difference, as the Bessi who were the most popular Thracian ethnic group, inveterate heathens and worshippers of Dionysus, had come to be associated with the umbrella ethnonym. Iustinus I (AD 518–527) was most probably Thracian as evident by the ethnic group to which he is said to belong and by his birthplace inWestern Thrace, and furthermore, by the explicit facts about the line of hereditary rulers of whom he was the progenitor. The best known of them was Iustinianus I (AD 527–565), his sister's son and the emperor to whom early Byzantium owes its grandeur, whereas his nephew Iustinus II (AD 565–578) adopted Tiberius Constantinus (AD 578–582) of whom there is reliable evidence that he was Thracian just like the others. Historical continuity and the cultural heritage of Antiquity are not to be measured in terms of the numbers of bearers, the facts of whose lives are well known. It was knowledge, experience and energy that were adopted. The new historical age that was set in motion in Southeastern Europe by Byzantium and from AD 681 onwards by Bulgaria is the most telling proof that the destinies of peoples are interrelated.

CHRONOLOGICAL TABLE OF THE BEST KNOWN THRACIAN DYNASTIES

ODRYSIAN DYNASTY
(earmly 5th-early 3rd Centuries BC)

Teres I
(c.490–464 BC)

Founded and consolidated the Odrysian Kingdom.

Sparadokos
(c. 464–444 BC)

Son of Teres I. Best known for his silver coins: tetradrachmas, drachmas and diobols.

Sitalkes
(c. 444–424 BC)

Son of Teres I. Under his reign the Odrysian Kingdom had its greatest territorial expansion.

Maesades

Probably the third son of Teres I.Paradynast (co-ruler) of the region around Propontis (the Sea of Marmara).

Satokos
(end 5th Century BC)

Son of Sitalkes. Facts about his life are not available. Thucydides mentioned him twice. His name was engraved on two silver vessels from the Rogozen treasure.

Seuthes I
(424–407/405 BC)

Son of Sparadokos, married to the daughter of the Macedonian ruler Alexander I. Thucydides mentioned him; silver coins – didrachmas and drachmas – feature him.

Metokos
(407/405–389/386 BC)

Son or brother of Satokos. He minted bronze and silver coins.

Saratokos
(c. 400–390 BC)

Probably brother of Metokos. Depicted only on several types of silver coins with a low face value.

Hebryzelmis
(389–386–383 BC)

Probably son of Seuthes I or of paradynast Seuthes II who was son of Maesades. Mentioned by Xenophon. Minted bronze coins.

Kotys I
(383–359 BC)

Probably son of Seuthes I. Minted bronze and silver coins.

Amatokos
(359–351 BC)

Son of Metokos. Minted bronze coins.

Teres II
(351–342/341 BC)

Son of Amatokos. Minted bronze coins.

Kersebleptes
(359–341 BC)

Son of Kotys I. Minted bronze coins. In 341 Philip II of Macedon defeated him and his kingdom lost independence.

Berisades

Parentage unknown – probably son of Seuthes II or of Saratokos. After the death of Kotys I in 359 BC the Odrysian Kingdom was divided among three-rulers: Kersebleptes, Amatokos and Berisades, the latter receiving the lands locked between the rivers Mesta and Strouma. His rule was very short and no coins have been discovered so far related to him.

necropolis near Varna. More than 3,000 23.5-carat gold objects of the late 4th millennium BC, weighing 6.5 kg, have been found. Archaeological Museum, Varna

The gold treasure found at the village of Vulchitrun near Pleven. Consists of 13 vessels used in cult rituals. A most remarkable monument of the Late Bronze Age in Thrace (13th-12th C. BC). National Museum of History, Sofia.

Orpheus playing the lyre to Thracians wearing typical striped capes. Attic red-figure krater (5th C. BC). Altes Museum, Berlin

Figurative painting on the dome of the vault near Kazanluk. The most important Thracian monument of the late 4th C. and the first quarter of the 3rd C. BC. The Odrysian King Seuthes III is believed to have been buried there

A tombstone to Deines, son of Anaxander, made in Apollonia (late 6th C. BC). A masterpiece of Ionian monumental gravestones. National Museum of History, Sofia

A gold rhyton shaped like an
Amazon's head.
Panagyurishte Treasure (late
4th-early 3rd C. BC)

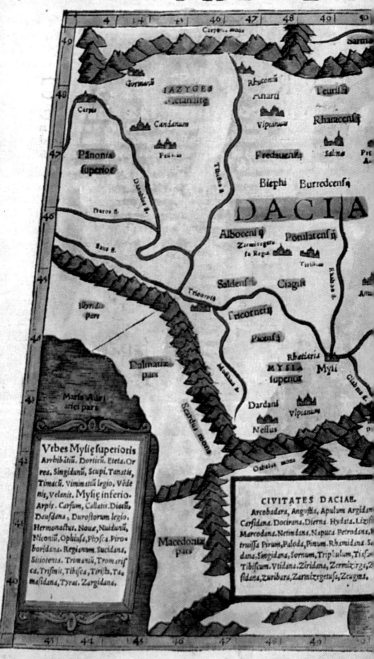

Vrbes Myliᴈ superioris
Arribibátiu. Doricū. Eteta. Oprea. Singidunū, Scupi. Tanatis. Timacū. Viminatiū legio, Vedenis, Velanis. Myliᴈ inferioris. Arpis. Carsum, Calliatis. Diacū, Deusdena, Durostorum legio. Hermonactiu. Nouᴈ, Nuidunū, Niconiū, Ophiusᴈ, Physca. Piroboridana. Regianum. Sucidana. Sitiotensa. Trimaniū, Tromarisca, Trisnis, Tibisca, Tirisia, Tamasidana, Tyrat. Zargidana.

CIVITATES DACIAE.
Arcobadara, Angustis, Apulum Argidaua
Cersidana. Docirans. Dierna. Hydata. Lizisi
Marcodana. Netinȗins. Napuca Petrodans,
truissa Pirum, Paloda, Pinum. Rhemidana. S
dana, Singidaua, Sornum, Triphulum, Tisa
Tibiscum. Vtidana. Ziridana, Zermizirgi, Z
sidana, Zuribara, Zarmizegetusa, Zeugma.

THRACIAE CIVITATES.
Abdera, Anchialus, Aphrodisia, Apræ
colonia, Bergula, Bisantha, Byzia, Car
pudemum, Cabyla, Cypsella. Deuela
tus, Dyma, Drusipara, Heraclia. Lysi
machia. Nicopolis. Ostaphus, Optsæ
na, Orcelis. Peronticum, Prasidium,
Philippo polis, Pergamum, Plotinopo
lis. Sardica. Torzi, Topiris, Traianopolis. Valla. Cherso. Calliopolis,
Cardia, Eleus.

,,A map of Thrace by Claudius Ptolemy, according to his
Geography''
    published by Sebastian Münster and Henricus Petri. Basle (1542)

The latest treasure of 165 silver vessels (20 kg), found at the village of Rogozen near Vratsa. National Museum of History, Sofia

The Thracian deity Heros (marble). More than 3,000 equestrian figures of Heros have been found. 2nd-3rd C. Museum of History, Stara Zagora

The old metropolitante in Nessebur. A Christian church (5th C.)

A Bulgarian warrior depicted on a gold jug of the Nagy-Szent-Miklos treasure, Romania, 9th C. The treasure con-sists of 23 vessels. Museum of art and history, Vienna.

A bas-relief carved in the rocks at the village of Madara, near Shoumen

A ceramic tile with an evangelical inscription in the Cyrillic alphabet. Archaeological Museum, Preslav

St Kliment of Ohrid: fresco (1295), St Kliment's Church, Ohrid

Ketriporis
(357/356–352/351 BC)

One of the sons of Berisades who succeeded him. Minted bronze coins. Defeated by Philip II of Macedon.

Seuthes III
(c. 330–302/301
or c. 297 BC)

Probably son of Kotys I and brother of Kersebleptes. He reestablished the Odrysian state and founded a new capital which was named after him, Seuthopolis (in the proximity of what is the town of Kazanluk today). Minted several types of bronze coins.

Spartokos
(c. 323–279/277)

Probably grandson of Kersebleptes. Resided in Cabile (in the proximity of what is the town of Yambol today). Mentioned in the great inscription of Seuthopolis. Minted one type of bronze coin between 281–279/277 BC.

Skostokos
(c. 277–255/250 BC)

Probably son of Spartokos. Resided in Cabile. Known from bronze and silver coins.

THRACIAN RULER FROM THE 2ND CENTURY BC

Mostis
(c. 120–100 BC)

Probably from the Odrysian dynasty. Minted several types of bronze coins and silver tetradrachmas. Mentioned on a stone inscription at today's Tekir Dag (ancient Byzante) on the Sea of Marmara.

ODRYSIAN (ODRYSIAN-ASTEIAN) DYNASTY
FROM THE 1ST CENTURY BC

Kotys
(c. 100–87 BC)

Sadalas I
(87–57 BC)

Kotys   Son of Sadalas I
(57–48 BC)

Sadalas II   Son of Kotys
(48–42 BC)

SAPEIAN DYNASTY
(second half of the 1st Century BC-mid 1st Century AD)

Rhaskuporis I   Son of the Sapeian ruler Kotys.
(48–42 BC)   Initially the Sapeians lived in
                           and dominated the lands locked
                           between the rivers Mesta and
                           Maritza along the northern Ae-
                           gean Sea coast. After the death
                           of the Odrysian ruler Sadalas
                           (48–42 BC) the Sapeian dy-
                           nasty moved to Bizye (today
                           Vize in European Turkey). Be-
                           fore that Bizye was the capital
                           of the last Odrysian (Odrysian-
                           Asteian) rulers.

Kotys   Son of Rhaskuporis I. Minted
(42–16 BC)   two types of bronze coins. Men-
                           tioned in several inscriptions.

Roemetalkas   Son of Kotys. Minted several
(16 BC–12 AD)   types of bronze coins and sil-
                           ver drachmas. Client ruler of
                           Octavius Augustus.

Kotys
(12–19 AD)

Son of Roemetalkas I. Married to Antonia Tryphaina, princess of Bosporus. Murdered by his uncle Rhaskuporis I.

Rhaskuporis II
(12–19 AD)

Son of Kotys and brother of Roemetalkas I. After the death of Roemetalkas in 12 AD Octavius Augustus divided Thrace in two and Kotys, son of Roemetalkas I, governed the one half and Rhaskuporis II, brother of Roemetalkas I, governed the other half. In 19 AD Rhaskuporis II murdered his nephew Kotys for which the Romans sent him into exile to Alexandria in Egypt where he was murdered shortly after.

Roemetalkas II
(19–37 AD)

Son of Rhaskuporis II. Bronze coins, whose typology is similar to the coins of Roemetalkas I, are attributed to him.

Roemetalkas III
(37–45 AD)

One of the three sons of Kotys who was killed in 19 AD. He was brought up and educated in Rome. Confidant of the Roman Emperor Caligula. In 45 AD he was killed as a consequence of internal revolts and conspiracy. In the same year the Roman Emperor Claudius made Thrace a Roman province.

RULERS OF THE TRIBALLI

Hales   Mentioned in ancient sources in
                            a campaign of Triballi to Ab-
                            dera, a city on the Aegean Sea
                            (c. 376/375 BC).

Didykaimos   Probably a dynast of the Tri-
                            balli from c. 4th Century BC.
                            His name was deciphered on a
                            silver vessel from the Rogozen
                            treasure.

Syrmos   Mentioned by Arianus as a
                            leader of the Triballi during the
                            campaign of Alexander the
                            Great in Thrace in 335 BC.

RULERS OF THE GETAI-DAKOI

Kothelas   Getan ruler from c. mid-4th
                            Century BC   with whom
                            Philip II of Macedon made an
                            alliance against the Scythian
                            ruler Ateasin 339 BC, and
                            married his daughter Meda.

Dromichaetes   Getan ruler with whom Lisy-
(end 4th-early 3rd   machus waged war.
Century BC)

Dromichaetes   Probably a Getan prince men-
(c. mid 3rd Century BC)   tioned in the records of the
                            Syrian ruler Antiochus II in
                            Thrace.

Moskon   Probably a Getan ruler, known
(3rd Century BC ?)   only from silver didrachmas.

Zaimodegikos   Getan ruler mentioned in an in-
(end 3rd Century BC)   scription from Istria.

Zoltes
(c. early 2nd Century BC)

Mentioned in an inscription from Istria.

Isanthes
(second half of the 3rd Century BC)

Chieftain of the Krobyzoi in the community of the Getai. Famous for his wealth and luxury.

Dromichaetes
(c. 87 BC)

Led a detachment of Thracians, ally to Mitridates VI Eupatorus.

Burebistas
(c. 62/55–44 BC)

Created a vast Getan state loc ked between the Carpathian Mountains and the western shores of the Black Sea.

Dicineus(=Dekaineos)
(c. mid 1st Century BC)

Contemporary of Burebistas, and a priest who probably succeeded him.

Comosicus
(second half of the 1st Century BC)

Getan king and priest who succeeded Dicineus.

Scorylo

According to Jordannes he ruled the Getai-Dakoi over the course of forty years.

Koson (= Cotison)
(44/43–c. 30/25 BC)

Dacian ruler. His name has been transcribed mistakenly as Cotison by several ancient authors. Koson is the correct name which was engraved on gold coins whose iconography was directly borrowed from a type of the silver coins of Brutos. For the time being these are the only gold coins coimng from a Thracian ruler.

Thiamarkos
(c. 30/25-c. 5 BC)

Probably the successor of Koson. His name occurs only in two short inscriptions on two ceramic vessels from excavations of the ancient village of Buridava (Romania). The title of king stands with his name.

Dikomes

Getan ruler who fought at Actium in 31 BC as an ally of Mark Antony against Octavius Augustus.

Roles
(c. 30–20 BC)

Getan ruler whose lands are believed to have been between the cities of Rousse and Silistra (NE Bulgaria). Ally of the Roman general Marcus Licinius Crassus the Younger against Bastarni and other Getan rulers who were hostile to Rome.

Dapyx

Getan ruler. Enemy of Roles and of Crassus who defeated him.

Zyraxes

Getan ruler residing in Genukia, a fort that has not been placed. He was defeated by Roles and Marcus Licinius Crassus the Younger who had joined forces.

Decebalus
(=Dekebalos)
(AD 87–106)

Son of Skorylo. The last and best known king of the Dakoi. He saved the integrity of the Dacian state from the legions of Emperor Domitianus. Emperor Trajanus defeated him in two successive wars (AD 101–102 and 105–106).

IV. A NEW STAR RISES ABOVE
THE   BALKANS

Year 681 of the Christian Era. The Foundation

It was Year of Grace 680. Constantinople, the magnificent capital of the Byzantine Empire, was a scene of theological disputes again. Theologians contested a deviation from the Orthodox faith. The Sixth Ecumenical Council was convened for that purpose and Emperor Constantine IV (668–685) took an active part in it. The purity of the Orthodox faith was saved but a prosaic event suddenly interrupted the wise debate.

As a matter of fact a rebellious people, *the Bulgars of Khan Asparuh*, had been causing trouble at the delta of the river Danube for some dozen of years already. As a result of the vicissitudes of history they had moved away from the tribal core in the northern Pontic steppe to seek a new homeland in legitimate Byzantine territories. All the resistance put up by the Byzantine garrisons in the forts was in vain. What was most terrible was that the Bulgars entered into close relations with another large barbarian people, *the Slavs*, whom the Empire suffered from for centuries. It was exactly the reason behind the Byzantine Emperor's decision to abandon his ecclesiastical affairs and undertake a difficult and risky campaign in the Danube delta.

Byzantium and the Bulgars had already had encounters. For many years that nomadic tribe had a common border with the Eastern Roman Empire west of the Caucasus. Centuries before the Proto-Bulgarians inhabited the far east lands of Asia. They were part of the great *Hunnic Alliance* which was permanently at war with its southern neighbour, the *Chinese Empire*. The rivalry continued till the 1st Century AD when the Chinese defeated the Huns and drove them westwards. The war laid the beginning of *the Great Migration of Peoples* that changed the destinies of civilizations. The Bulgars' trek was part of that Great Migration.

The trek to Europe was long and painful. They left their native land in Western Siberia around the river Irtysh, crossed the Tian Shan Mountains and made for the Ural Mountains. For some 150 years the Bulgars lived along the great Amu-Darya and Syr-Darya rivers. Their neighbours the Ugortsi were the first to bring the forefathers of the modern Bulgarians in touch with the magnificent Iranian civilization.

For almost a century they stayed in the steppes of Kazakhstan that matched well their nomadic style of life. However, the never-ending waves of incoming peoples pushed them westwards. So around the 5th Century the Bulgars settled in the Ciscaucasus and along the northern Black Sea coast. In that period they came in touch with the Iranian-cultured Alans and this left an imprint on their further development.

Contemporary archaeologists have come across the remains of an interesting culture which thrived in the Azov region between the 6th and the 10th Centuries. It was named the Saltovo-Maytsk culture after the centres where it was located. As a matter of fact it was the combination of Bulgar traditions with the Sarmatian and Alan style of life. For the Bulgars the 6th Century was a time of gradual settlement although the nomadic spirit was still powerful. The necropoli which have been brought to light show how the steppe warriors were buried together with their war horses, weapons and insignia. These burial rites have helped an assessment of anthropological characteristics of the Bulgars. Theirs were Europoid with slight Mongoloid features acquired as a result of long contact with the Turkic peoples.

The Bulgars created their first state that Byzantium called *Old Great Bulgaria* in the first half of the 7th Century. *Khan Kubrat* was its founder and it was locked between the rivers Kuban, Dnieper, Donets and the Sea of Azov and the Black Sea. The Byzantines knew that ruler well. In 635 Emperor Heraclius concluded a peace treaty with him and conferred on him the title "patrician". When in the 670s the great Khan died, his belongings all made of solid gold were laid in his grave. These were feast vessels, a sword with a gold casing, a buckle insignia for a belt and rings presented by the Basileus with a Byzantine title engraved on them. These precious finds are now in The Hermitage in St. Petersburg as the most magnificent funeral offerings to a nomadic chieftain from the period in question.

Old Great Bulgaria did not exist for a long time. Soon it fell apart under the blows of the Khazars, another large barbarian people. It was under their pressure that some of the Bulgars migrated to the north along the valley of the river Volga where later they founded a new state. A group remained in the old place and surrendered to the suzerainty of the Khazar khagan. Another group of the tribe led by Khan Asparuh who was the youngest son of Khan Kubrat set out for the Balkan Peninsula.

In 680 Byzantium already knew what the *Slavs* were like. They were previously known to the Romans, as the Roman emperors failed to conquer the border regions. Roman authors from the lst–2nd Centuries – Pliny the Elder, Tacitus and Ptolemy – called them collectively *Venedi* and wrote that the vast and unexplored lands north of the Carpathian Mountains were their homeland.They had a very vague idea about them and described their practices as close to those of the *Germanic* tribes.

Archaeological excavations nowadays substantially support the scanty facts from history. The *Pshevorsk* culture that existed in the lst–4th Centuries in the regions that the Roman authors describe is believed to be the earliest Slav culture. Two other cultures considered to be early Slav cultures, those of *Zarubinetsk* and *Chernyakhovsk*, took shape to the east and southeast of the Pshevorsk cultural area. Translated in modern geographic terms these are today's Ukraine and Belarus. It is interesting to note that these archaeological cultures were collective and a product of the ancient Slav and also Germanic, Sarmatian and some other tribes.

About the 4th Century AD the main Slav groups were clearly distinguished by contemporary authors: the Eastern group (the Anti), the Western group (the Venedi) and the Southern group (the Slavenes). These groups were tossed in the whirl of the Great Migration of Peoples. In the late 5th and early 6th Centuries the Southern Slav group started systemic incursions into the Balkan Peninsula, towards its interior.

In those days the old Roman border along the Danube was in a deplorable state after the numerous barbarian invasions. The onetime strong cities *Oescus, Nove, Ratiaria* and others were abandoned in ruins. The Emperor Iustianianus I (527–565) tried to reinforce the border by putting up hundreds of new forts along the range of Haemus (today Stara Planina). He did it only partially because of the never-ending Slav waves sweeping the Empire.

The Byzantine emperors found it was beyond their capacity to fight with the Slavs. The latter were not an organised army that one might battle with normally but huge masses of people invading the state from the north. Inspired by the thought of Byzantine wealth the Slavs chose to raid cities like Thessalonica. However the Slav settlement all over the Balkans down to the Peloponnes scared Byzantium a lot more. Byzantine authors were grieved to note that the Empire was being Slavicised.

Archaeological studies recreate what the numerous poor Slav villages along the Danube were like. These were organised in the proximity of the declining Byzantine cit-

Justinian

ies. Ultimately the Empire had to swallow their presence. This is how the situation looked when the well organised mounted Bulgars arrived.

The strong Byzantine army left Constantinople in the spring of 680. Some of the troops made a land crossing while the core troops led by the Emperor Constantine IV disembarked at the Danube delta. On seeing how numerous these were, the Bulgars and their allies, the Slav detachments, retreated to the *fort Onglos*. In the next couple of days the Byzantines did not attack and the troops were demoralised. The culminating point was when a gout attack suffered by the Emperor sent him away with courtiers to the nearby spa in Mesembria.

Khan Asparuh seized that excellent opportunity. Taking advantage of the rumour of the Emperor's flight he delivered a mortal blow to the Byzantine armies. The defeated troops were chased down to *Odessos* (today's Varna). Most of the Byzantines were killed or taken prisoner of war and the news of the terrible defeat spread fast round the Empire. In the next couple of months the Khan of the Bulgars took the trouble to polish relations of alliance with the Slavs and was involved in several blitz operations south of the Stara Planina.

Thus all of a sudden the Byzantine Empire was forced to comply. In the summer of 681 Constantine IV had to conclude a peace treaty with the Bulgars and, to quote a contemporary who recorded the events in a chronicle, an annual tribute was to be paid according to the terms of the treaty which was a "*disgrace to Romans*". A new star, the state of Bulgars and Slavs, rose above the Balkans. Theirs was the first barbarian kingdom that scarred the face of the Eastern Roman Empire in what used to be the province of Moesia Inferior north of the eastern chain of Haemus. The future was to be one of rivalry and wars between the two states but also of cultural and economic cooperation.

The life and death struggle for the throne in the 8th Century

In the late 7th and early 8th Centuries the Byzantine Empire fell prey to the numerous Arab armies raiding it from the east, the incessant fight for the throne and the never-ending church strife. In these circumstances the Bulgars managed to consolidate their state. They reinforced their relations with the Slavs and, when needed, resorted to force to make the Slav tribes obedient. In the first half of the 8th Century the borders were all ramparts and trenches stretching for hundreds of miles. Forts (auls) dotted the country. However it was not just Byzantium which threatened the young state. Two powerful khaganates, those of the Khazars and of the Avars, posed a constant threat from the north. The Khazars, the inveterate enemies of the Bulgars, were particularly fierce. The founder of the state Khan Asparuh was killed in battle when one of their many raids was repulsed. It took his son *Tervel* who succeeded him some two decades to consolidate his rule and he even interfered in the Byzantine Empire's internal affairs.

The dynastic problem which no monarchy has escaped cropped up a couple of years after his death. The *Doulo* royal family from which the founder Khan Asparuh descended had to share claims with the big Bulgar clans *Vokil* and *Ugain*. All this was contemporaneous with the consolidation of the Byzantine Empire. The Emperor in Constantinople, Constantine V Copronymus (741–775), became a fierce enemy to the new state. He led nine campaigns against Bulgaria within 20 years on land and sea, the only objective being to wipe Bulgaria off the face of the earth.

The Byzantine Emperor was a treacherous but experienced enemy. He did not count on military operations alone; in addition he had a network of spies in *Pliska*, the royal city of Bulgaria (at today's Shumen in Northeast

Bulgaria). The Palace of the Khan was teeming with spies who provoked the emergence of two hostile parties. One was in favour of close relations with Byzantium and the other insisted on a hard line against the Empire. Khans came and went, some of whom ruled for a couple of days only. Records mention briefly *Vineh*, *Telets, Sabin, Umor,Toktu* and *Pagan*. What is known for sure is that some of them died a violent death – either stabbed or poisoned by the other party's henchmen.

Khan Telerig (772–777) tried to enforce law and order. He was the first after a long interruption to pursue an active policy with neighbours. Most interesting of all is his clever move when he feigned loyalty to the Emperor and asked him to provide the names of his closest friends from the pro-Byzantine party. On getting them the Khan immediately ordered that all traitors be arrested and executed regardless of their social status. The Emperor Constantine V Copronymus was shocked by this outrage and died of apoplexy during a punitive campaign against Bulgaria. Khan Telerig, though, fell victim to plotting courtiers. In 777 he abandoned the throne and fled to Constantinople to ask for refuge.

These events made an impression on the royal city of Pliska. Archaeological studies show that initially it was not a city in the ancient classical or modern sense of the word. Loyal to the old nomadic tradition the Bulgars established a *campos* (camp), encircled by fieldwork and covering 23 square kilometres. The campos was designed to give shelter to the whole horde and to all horses and cattle in days of trouble. Portable tents and the light-weight dwellings of the Bulgars were strewn on the lush pastures inside.

A solid stone fortification had been erected in the very centre of the area that was encircled by fieldwork c. the mid-8th Century. This was a solid castle with a rectangular plan, built of monoliths and covering 0.4 hectares. The roots of that architecture lead back to Asia Anterior and models of Antiquity. The castle was the fort of the Bulgarian khans. Nearby there was a palace that was not surrounded by a fence and its ruins have been exposed by archaeologists.

It was at the time of political strife that a secret tunnel connected the castle and the palace. No doubt it was an invisible passage that enabled rulers to move unnoticed in times of trouble. It is quite likely though that delegated murderers might have used it from time to time to sneak into the Khan's apartments. Whatever it was, the tunnel was not removed in the next century; moreover, a maze of such corridors was created in the centre of Pliska.

The political crisis came to an end under *Khan Kardam* (777–802). Cleverly he took advantage of the breakthrough of his predecessor and multiplied his successes.He was a ruler of firm will who crushed internal resistance and attacked Byzantium, which was rent by internecine strife again. In 791-792 Bulgaria and the Empire were at war again. Khan Kardam's armies moved south of the Stara Planina and met the imperial army in battle at *Marceli*, a fort near today's Karnobat in Eastern Bulgaria.This time the Byzantine troops suffered utter defeat and the Emperor's tent and treasure chest were seized in battle. The Emperor Constantine VI (780–797) had a narrow escape from the battlefield. This is how Bulgaria survived in the turbulent 8th Century and entered the new century surging and internationally recognized. However, new ordeals lay ahead.

Khan Omurtag (814–831) –
the statesman and builder

In the summer of 811 the royal city of Pliska was all fire and smoke. The 60,000-man strong army commanded by the Emperor Nicephorus I Genik (802–811) plundered and massacred and showed no mercy even for the young Bulgar children. *Khan Krum* (802–814), the successor of Kardam, watched this heart-breaking picture from a distance as he was short of men to fight the Byzantines.

He knew well that the Emperor was to cross the inaccessible ridges of Stara Planina on the way home. It was during that difficult return with so much unknown uncertainty that Khan Krum lay in ambush for the Byzantine army which was carrying piles of booty. The cream of Byzantine aristocracy was massacred in the hot July night and the Emperor, too, was slaughtered at the end. Following the old barbarian rite the Bulgarian ruler had his skull embossed with silver and gold and raised a toast drinking from this bowl.

Khan Krum was a wise and able ruler who not only won but also knew how to take advantage of victories. In 805 he enlarged Bulgaria which reached Central Europe by conquering Transylvania and Lower Pannonia and taking them away from the disintegrating Avar Khaganate. After the defeat of the Byzantines Khan Krum pursued a very active policy in the south. In the next two years he had several other brilliant victories and his armoured mounted men reached Constantinople. Initially they limited their raids to the environs of the capital of Byzantium but in 814 the Khan planned and prepared a campaign to conquer the city. The Byzantines were extremely happy when they heard the news of the ambitious ruler suffering a fatal heart attack on the eve of the campaign.

However their happiness was premature. His son *Khan Omurtag* who succeeded him became one of the most powerful European monarchs of the day. He combined military success with diplomacy even more successfully than his father. Khan Omurtag had other virtues to add required for the ideal medieval ruler: large-scale construction, law-making and patronage of the arts.

First he concluded a reliable 30-year peace treaty with Byzantium, incorporating his conditions in it. From then onwards he had no problems with the Empire as long as he reigned. Moreover, from time to time the Bulgarian Khan had a final say in the solution of Byzantium's domestic problems. In 823 Khan Omurtag was asked by the Emperor to help suppress the uprising of Thomas the Slavonian and the conditions of the peace treaty were reaffirmed in return.

The Bulgarian ruler was interested mostly in lands north of the Danube. Relations with the Khazars were dealt with on a lasting basis and after several battles the Khazars were no longer a threat to the Bulgarian state. Khan Omurtag's army reached the river Dnieper and conquered the area.

The eastern lands of the Avar Khaganate had already been conquered by Khan Krum. His son carried on and seized the big fortresses Belgrade, Branichevo and Sirmium. *The Frankish* offensive from the west delivered the mortal blow to the Avar state. Bulgaria and the Empire of the Franks had a common border running along the river Tisza exactly across the middle of what is today Budapest, the capital of Hungary. The Bulgars and Franks were involved in a couple of border conflicts, yet soon peace was established which continued during the reign of Omurtag's successors.

So Bulgaria became a European power. Its northern border stretched from the Dnieper to the middle reaches of the Danube and encompassed the Carpathian Mountains. To the west it incorporated what is Serbia today; to the south the border with Byzantium cut across the middle of Thrace.

In 814 Khan Omurtag found the capital Pliska all in ashes as his father simply had not had the time to rebuild it. This might have suggested the ambitious and large-scale construction effort which soon spread countrywide. First and foremost he changed the system of fortified auls that had existed under the previous rulers. The fortifications were surrounded by a rampart and moat, and tents and light-weight garrison quarters were located inside.

Khan Omurtag started the construction of sturdy stone forts. They had the same purpose for the location of troops but the barracks were built of stone and had every convenience. Mansions were built for the commanders which had bathrooms and heating.

Khan Omurtag's ideas of building came prominently to light when the centre was brought to light. Actually he had the remains of the previous fortified palace of khans dismantled and another pompous building erected on the site: a Throne Chamber. The apartments were enlarged by adding new premises to provide for convenience and ceremonies in the court. These were water tanks, baths, residence buildings and pagan temples. The whole complex was surrounded by a brick wall whose purpose was not defence but rather to be a screen so that mortals could not observe the life of the God-chosen.

Khan Omurtag was the ruler who made Pliska a city in the proper sense of the word. He had a large stone fortress built inside almost in line with the ancient fortification requirements. The thick wall was guarded by many regularly planned towers. The wall surrounded the Khan's Palace, the mansions of the aristocracy and the large squares paved with stone slabs. In addition to the above-mentioned maze of secret passages there was a water supply and sewerage system of clay pipes beneath.

The Bulgarian ruler had pompous buildings erected and decorated. Columns and statues brought from Byzantium were placed in the squares. Lions were chiselled out of

5.

stone on a pediment for one of the auls. For decades the Bulgars had been worshipping a huge bas relief featuring the victorious khan on horseback stamping a lion, presumably a symbol of the arch enemy, the Byzantine Empire, that had been transfixed by a spear. That scene was chiselled in the rocks in Madara, a cult centre that was not far from Pliska.

Dozens of monumental inscriptions from the time of Khan Omurtag have survived to date. These relate juridical and diplomatic treaties, stock taking of the ammunitions in whole army units, and official reports of construction sites. All these inscriptions are in Greek, the language used in the Khan's Chancellery. Although a pagan, that ruler was undoubtedly an enlightened man who was aware of the importance of the Christian Byzantine Empire for civilization. Little wonder that he had his engravers depict him with the insignia of a Christian king on a memorial gold medallion.

The great Khan was rent by internal controversy. Omurtag's major conquests and cultural policy associated him closely with Christian Europe. However, he was devoted to the religion of his predecessors and witch-hunted the Christians whose numbers were growing, including his own people. The Crown Prince *Enravota* was converted to Christianity and lost the throne because of that. Just like the Roman Emperor Diocletian Khan Omurtag's actions were bringing the triumph of Christian religion nearer and nearer against his own will. Yet another three decades were to elapse before the new religion triumphed.

V. THE THIRD EMPIRE IN EUROPE

Year 866 of the Christian Era. Conversion to Christianity

Khan Omurtag died, leaving a large, rich and well-organised state. This allowed his successors to conduct their policy in relative calm. *Khan Malamir* (831–836) and *Khan Persian* (836–852) gradually extended their borders, mainly southwards into the Byzantine Empire. The Byzantines' attempts to resist ended in failure and were followed by powerful counter-offensives. In 836 the Bulgars captured one of the Empire's biggest cities, Philippopolis (modern Plovdiv) and settled there. A year later Isbules, an experienced military leader, provoked a rebellion of the Slavic tribes in Macedonia and Aegean Thrace which were still dominions of the Byzantine Emperor. Then Isbules intervened with a strong army to occupy those important territories. Bulgaria kept pushing the Byzantines further southwards in the Balkan Peninsula.

The ethnic composition of the state changed dramatically as more and more Slavic tribes joined it. The Slavs already outnumbered the Bulgars, although the latter pulled all strings of power. The two ethnoses amalgamated slowly but irreversibly. This process was to end with the Bulgars' assimilation into the Slavic sea, to which they would give their name[1]. A new basis was needed for this, however: a common religion.

Difficulties in religious, political and military affairs, which had troubled Byzantium for a hundred and fifty years, were resolved in 843. The Arab threat was finally eliminated and the empire began to regain lost territory.

---

[1] Bulgarians: Same as former Bulgars (Translator's note)

The Byzantines launched an active European policy under the banner of Orthodoxy. Logically, they started with their northern neighbour Bulgaria.

It all began with a series of political and military failures by *Khan Boris* (852–889), the new ruler. In 853 he tried to intervene in, and take advantage of, conflicts in Western and Central Europe. Khan Boris sided with Charles II the Bald, King of the Franks, in his war against the German Kingdom. The Bulgarian ruler had set his sights on the land of the Croatians in the western part of the Balkan Peninsula. Away from the motherland, the Bulgarian army was defeated at a time when a German army invaded and pillaged Transylvania.

The Bulgarians thereafter sought to develop closer ties with the German Kingdom. One of the clauses of their treaty carried the obligation for Bulgarians to be baptised into the Roman Church. However, the events of 862–864 took place at lightning speed.

To start with, the Bulgarians were hit by a terrible natural disaster in the summer of 863. Towns and villages were struck by a devastating earthquake, followed by severe famine. The old enemy, the Byzantine Empire,was quick to take advantage and attacked Bulgaria by land and sea. Bulgaria needed peace at any cost and the price it paid was to adopt Christianity from Constantinople. Many priests arrived from the Byzantine capital to prepare the mass conversion. The Khan himself was baptised one night in 866.

More hardships lay in store for Bulgaria. The old aristocracy realised that conversion from paganism to Christianity would close the chapter of its hegemony. The aristocrats staged an uprising which was crushed with violence by Boris. Fifty-two aristocratic families, including women and children, were executed on the walls of Pliska, the capital city.

Granted the location of his state in Europe, the Bulgarian ruler did the one thing possible: he manoeuvred between East and West. In the next four years he recognised the supremacy of the Catholic Church, which sent its envoys to Bulgaria. The newly converted prince, who took the Christian name of Mihail, sent to the See of Rome a long list of questions about Christian morals and ethics. Pope Nicholas I (858–867) sent him an extensive benevolent reply which, having survived many vicissitudes in history, is a major source of information on the Bulgarians' life at the time.

Prince Boris-Mihail was set on gaining the greatest possible independence for his Church. His tactics were successful and Byzantium radically changed its attitude. At the eighth oecumenical council in 870 it proposed officially that Bulgaria should return to the bosom of the Patriarchate of Constantinople with the status of an independent metropolitan see. The Bulgarians accepted, an act which was of momentous consequence for the country's future.

In 889 the old prince stepped down and retired to a monastery where he could commune undisturbed with the new God. He was succeeded by the heir to the throne, *Vladimir-Rassate* (889–893). Then something unexpected happened. Like the Emperor Julian, who tried to re-establish paganism in the distant 4th Century and was called the Apostate, the new prince abandoned Christianity and reverted to the Bulgars' ancient pagan deities. Archaeological evidence suggests that he destroyed newly built churches and restored pagan temples.

Monk Boris-Mihail acted promptly and decisively. He left the monastery and convened a popular council with the help of his loyal aristocrats. Vladimir-Rassate was deposed and blinded. His place was taken by another son of Boris-Mihail's, Simeon. His training had been suited to his fine qualities and had prepared him to become a man of letters and a spiritual leader of the people. History, how-

ever, showed that he was destined to become one of the
greatest men of medieval Europe.

Simeon the Great (893–927): The King of Kings

Prince Simeon had graduated from the University of Constantinople, one of the most prestigious seats of learning at
the time. Well versed in ancient culture and the achievements of Christian civilisation, he proved to be a surprisingly good politician and military leader. However, the
credit for Bulgaria's great successes in that period should
not go entirely to him. In fact, the pagan khans Krum and
Omurtag had laid the groundwork for them and this process continued throughout the 9th Century. Simeon was
the man destined to crown the efforts of many a great
statesman.

The wars against the Byzantine Empire, which were entirely aggressive in nature, were an important characteristic of his reign. But there was more to Simeon's plans
than to do away with Byzantium. He knew by heart the
ancient theory of the state, which held that there could be
only one empire in the civilised world. Alexander the Great
had launched that idea, which was taken up by Rome and
then by the surviving eastern half of the huge empire. In
800, Charlemagne made the first attempt to overthrow
Byzantium, proclaiming himself Emperor of Rome.
Simeon the Great was the second European ruler to undertake this incredibly difficult and ambitious task.

A pretext to attack Byzantium was found in 894. Its
Emperor transferred trade with the Bulgarians from
Thessalonica to Constantinople, thus impeding commer-
cial contacts. Prince Simeon was quick to react and carried out several offensives southwards that same year.

In this early campaign, however, the Bulgarian ruler
underestimated the enemy and overrated his own strength.

He won the battles indeed, but the Byzantines enticed the Hungarians to make a surprise attack from the north. The latter were part of a successive wave of the great people's migration and were looking for a new land to settle.

With all Bulgarian forces fighting in the south, there was no one at the outset to stop the Hungarians from laying waste the north of the country. Then, with their enemies the Pechenegs on his side, Simeon countered the blow. In 896 the Hungarians were crushed by the allies and moved on to Central Europe where they founded their state. Having dealt with this problem, Simeon mounted a lightning attack on Thrace and defeated the Byzantine army at Bulgarophygon near Constantinople.

The Byzantine Empire put up resistance for a few more years until finally in 904 it had to sign a disadvantageous peace treaty. By moving trade back to Thessalonica it virtually recognised Bulgaria's territorial gains in Eastern Thrace, Macedonia and Albania. The terms of the peace treaty were extremely disagreeable to Byzantium and extended the Bulgarian borders deep into the south. Simeon's strategic goals did not end there, however.

An excellent opportunity to intervene in the Empire's affairs presented itself in 912. Prince Simeon led a huge army to Constantinople on the specious pretext of helping the Emperor, then a minor, to oust his uncle who had usurped the throne. The army laid siege to Constantinople which forced Byzantium to recognise Simeon as Tsar of the Bulgarians and consent to a marriage between the underage Emperor Constantine VII (913–959) and Simeon's younger daughter. The marriage brought Simeon the title of "father of the Emperor". This was the ultimate aim of the campaign because now Simeon was entitled to intervene in Byzantine affairs at will and even to occupy the throne as first regent of the Emperor. All he had to do was wait for the right time. Simeon was already within sight of his easy lawful ascent to the position of "King of Kings", as was the full title of the rulers of the Eastern Roman Empire.

Of course, clever people in Constantinople saw through the designs of the Bulgarian ruler. As early as 914 the treaty was cancelled. Arms had the final say. The two sides spent the next three years making preparations. Tsar Simeon had no problems in Thrace and his soldiers criss-crossed Byzantine territory as far as Constantinople. The Byzantines, for their part, were getting ready for the decisive battle as they had done in the 8th Century in the fateful combats with the Arabs. Troops from all over Asia Minor were called up and the aristocrats pledged to die for their country.

The great battle was fought at the Achelous River (on the Black Sea) on August 20, 917. It was one of the biggest medieval battles, with hundreds of thousands of people involved. Those killed numbered in the order of tens of thousands. Byzantine historians were unanimous that it was the worst bloodshed in several centuries. Heaps of human bones lay bleaching in the sun by the small river for half a century.

Bulgaria won a resounding victory in the hand-to-hand battle. The Byzantine army suffered an overwhelming defeat in which most soldiers were killed. Tsar Simeon was without a rival in the Balkan Peninsula. He, however, did not have a strong fleet, which was crucial if he was to conquer Constantinople. In the next few years he repeatedly tried to establish contact and secure ships from the powerful Arab caliphs, but his dream never materialised in his lifetime.

Still, he achieved many of his goals. In 918 the Bulgarian church was proclaimed a patriarchate, the first officially recognised in the Orthodox world after the traditional patriarchates of Constantinople, Jerusalem, Antioch and Alexandria. Three centres of spiritual power were established in Europe: the Pope, the Oecumenical Patriarch and the Patriarch of Bulgaria. Failing to obtain the title of Byzantine Emperor by diplomatic moves, Simeon took it by force. In 918 he again was crowned Tsar, this time by the Bulgarian Patriarch. In documents of that time Simeon is referred to as "the Emperor of the Byzantines", i.e. of the Eastern Roman Empire, the first among the European rulers of his time.

Simeon made his mark in politics as a typical Machiavellian ruler. He possessed the qualities of the ideal ruler described by Niccolo Machiavelli in the 16th Century. Six hundred years earlier, the Bulgarian Tsar answered the description. He combined the qualities of an experienced diplomat and a great military leader, as evidenced by his correspondence with the rulers of the Empire. This view is corroborated by contemporary historians. They are unanimous that along with Charlemagne, Simeon was the first ruler of a barbarian state in Europe who turned it into a great power on the Continent. Not only did he make conquests, but he also managed to legitimise them.

Tsar Simeon died of a heart attack in 927 at the height of a new military campaign against Byzantium. He left Bulgaria the third Christian empire in Europe: rich, powerful and large. But Simeon would not have qualified as a Machiavellian ruler if it were not for one very important quality: he was a patron and lover of culture and education. That is why his reign is also known as the Golden Age of medieval Bulgaria.

The Golden Age

It cannot be said that before they adopted Christianity the Bulgars had not been in contact with the world civilisations. In Central Asia and Asia Anterior the nomads who had joined the great people's migration came in contact with Iranian culture. Traces of this high art and reli-

gion can be found in a number of Bulgarian monuments
dating back to pagan times. As for the Slavs, they had bordered on the Roman Empire for centuries. Settlement in
the Balkan Peninsula and contacts with Byzantine
civilisation gave a fresh impetus to various cultural processes. However, the new world religion was increasingly
being seen as an important prerequisite for communication with other peoples.

On the other hand, the adoption of Christianity lent ur-
gency to the issue of preserving the Bulgarians' national
identity in the face of encroachments by Constantinople
and Rome. The invention of the Slavic alphabet and its
introduction in Bulgaria played a surprisingly important
role in this respect.

It all began with a campaign launched by the Byzantine Empire, which had made its foreign policy more in-
tensive since the council of 843. Orthodox missionaries
spearheaded the campaign for the dissemination of Byzantine influence and toured the places subject to
Christianisation. Two of the missionaries, the brothers
Cyril and Methodius, who came from Thessalonica, were
highly educated and held a prominent position in Byzantine society. They had accomplished a number of important missions when all of a sudden they retired to a remote monastery and set themselves an incredibly challenging task: to invent an alphabet for the Slav peoples.

There is no indisputable evidence in source-books that
they were of Slavic origin. Furthermore, it is not known
who proposed the idea: the brothers themselves or the Byzantine government. Historical logic points to the latter as-
sumption. It was no coincidence that having invented the
alphabet, the two brothers left for Rome and Central Europe where the rising Eastern Roman Empire bore the brunt
of the battle for the people.

This "cold war" was really daunting. The future of
millions of Slavs wavering between Constantinople and

Rome was at stake. The brothers themselves burned out in the battle: Cyril died in 869 and Methodius in 885. Yet, in several decades of hard work they had drawn in and trained more than 200 disciples. After the teachers died, their followers were brutally persecuted. Some were sold into bondage, while others roamed around Europe homeless.

That is how things stood when, in 866, the newly baptised Prince Boris-Mihail invited the disciples to Bulgaria.This was part of a well-considered policy. The Bulgarian ruler turned the tables on the Byzantines, using their own ideological weapon.

Things developed on an impressive scale under Simeon. Cyril and Methodius's disciples were sent to the four corners of the vast state. They worked zealously in Northern Bulgaria, Thrace, Macedonia and north of the Danube, in Transylvania. Naum, Kliment and Angelary were particularly active. Apart from teaching, many of the larger group of disciples headed the Bulgarian spiritual institutions to become church leaders.

At first more translations of religious books were made, much needed in the young Christian state. Thanks to the excellent education he had received in Constantinople, Simeon took an active part himself. His contemporaries were unanimous that he was a book-loving tsar, which was not just courtly flattery. Moreover, apart from organising the literary scene, Simeon authored literary works.

A second wave of men of letters began under the guidance of Cyril and Methodius's disciples. Along with Bishop Konstantin, Methodius's old disciple, younger scholars such as John the Exarch and Monk Hrabr worked in the new capital Veliki Preslav. They wrote the first original Slavic literary works.

Konstantin of Preslav wrote the remarkable *Edifying Gospel*, a collection of homilies, lectures and other Christian material. Its most interesting features are the first Old Bulgarian poems and a short chronicle of historic events.

Unlike him, John the Exarch studied the world from a philosophical point of view. In many respects his *Hexameron* is relevant even now. It is based on Aristotelian philosophical knowledge and the writings of the Christian theologians of the lst–5th Century AD, and includes John the Exarch's own insights. In line with the ancient conception of philosophy as a general science, *the Hexameron* contains various observations from the realms of medicine and natural science. A detailed description of Veliki Preslav and its buildings provides clues to archaeologists nowadays.

Monk Hrabr wrote an apologia for Slavic letters. All kinds of writings including heretical literature banned by the church and historical works, circulated in the 10th and llth Centuries. Presbyter Kozma distinguished himself by writing an emotional homily against the new heresies.

In the Golden Age of Tsar Simeon men of letters wrote many more Old Bulgarian literary works. From Bulgaria literature circulated quickly among the Slavs, hungry for writings in their own tongue. This made the work of Boris-Mihail and Simeon, who gave refuge to the persecuted Slavic enlighteners, very important.

Tsar Simeon and, to an even greater extent, his son *Tsar Peter* (927–968) did much to develop their towns, especially the capital Veliki Preslav. It was central to their doctrine of power as a counterpoint to the Byzantine capital Constantinople. Ideologically, the town was designed in opposition to the centre of the Empire.

The new capital was built on the site of a fortress dating from the time of Khan Omurtag. The idea to move the centre of the state emerged during the reign of Tsar Boris-Mihail and was probably linked to the adoption of Christianity. An official decision was taken at the council in 893 which brought Simeon to the throne. His name and rule are associated with the major construction works inVeliki Preslav.

To begin with, the stone walls of the old stronghold were extended considerably. A new stone wall was built on the outside, enclosing an area of five square kilometres which was enormous by the standards of the time. This was where the town proper stood, with hundreds of rich residences of secular and ecclesiastical aristocrats. Similar mansions were built within a radius of dozens of kilometres around Veliki Preslav in imitation of aristocratic villas and monasteries in the environs of Constantinople.

The main likeness was sought in the great palace of the Bulgarian tsars. The sacred palace of the Byzantine emperors built by Constantine the Great (324–337) in the Byzantine capital was ranked among the wonders of the world. Dozens of churches, monumental buildings, squares and galleries formed an ensemble surrounded by a separate wall and provided a backdrop for the extremely intricate court ceremonies. In 800 Charlemagne claimed to dominate the world but never so much as thought of building such a city in his state.

This task was undertaken by the ambitious Bulgarian rulers. Excavations have shown that one more fortress with a massive stone wall was put up at the heart of the large inner fortification at the end of the 9th Century and the first half of the 10th Century. It has not been fully studied yet, although excavations have now been going on for a hundred years. The spacious ornate rooms of the Tsar and the Patriarch, monumental buildings, churches and heated baths have been unearthed. They stand in vast flagstoned squares, in which marble fountains and foundations of triumphal columns have been found. The buildings were connected by colonnaded galleries, which once sheltered people from the sun and the rain. Hundreds of stone masons, mosaicists, artists and glass-blowers decorated all those buildings. The floors of the palaces were covered with mosaics of coloured marble pieces which, according to contemporaries, resembled flower-strewn meadows. Looking up, one could see imposing colonnades and richly ornamented marble cornices.The walls were faced with decorative marble tiles or panels in the Preslav style, an art brought from the east and developed in Bulgaria in the 10th Century. Tiles, icons,whole iconostases and pots were made of fine white clay, using a sophisticated pre-faience technology.

In its heyday, Veliki Preslav had hundreds of thousands of inhabitants. It was the undisputed centre of Slavdom in the 9th and 10th Centuries. Along with Constantinople and the towns of the Omayyads in Spain after the Arab conquest, it was one of the hubs of civilisation. It should be remembered that at the time today's great European centres, Paris and London, were turning slowly from villages into towns and stone architecture was still an exotic rarity and a luxury few could afford.

The Byzantine Empire strikes back (971–1018)

The Byzantine Empire grew considerably stronger in the second half of the 10th Century and went on the offensive on all fronts. The most intense military campaigns were launched by the warrior emperors Nicephorus II Phocas (963–969) and John I Tzimisces (969–976). The Byzantine armies invaded Mesopotamia, Syria and Lebanon, all of which had been conquered by the Arabs back in the 7th and 8th Centuries. Byzantine flags flew over the great towns of Antioch, Baalbek, Beirut and Sidon.

Meanwhile, Bulgarian military power was on the wane. Nevertheless, the economy and culture of the vast Bulgarian Empire flourished, reaching unprecedented heights. However, a strictly observed 40-year peace with Byzantium undermined the vitality of the victors. The subjugated Serbs, Hungarians and Pechenegs, who were vassals of the Bulgarians, rose in arms. Unlike his father, the highly educated Tsar Peter was not a warrior.

The knot of serious problems came to a head in 968 when he retired to monastic life and his son *Boris II* (968–971) mounted the throne. This coincided with a massive invasion of the Balkan Peninsula by the strong Russian Prince Svyatoslav. The large army of the northern barbarians overran Northeastern Bulgaria twice, in 968 and 969. The Russians liked the rich Bulgarian land very much and Prince Svyatoslav made no secret of his intention to settle there.

The Bulgarians were forced to arrange a hasty truce on unfavourable terms. That is when the Byzantine Empire struck. Following several preparatory operations, in April 971 John Tzimisces laid siege to Veliki Preslav. The capital, surrounded by thick fortified walls, was conquered without much difficulty because the Bulgarians lacked the motivation and drive to put up resistance. In subsequent battles with the Byzantines, Russian garrisons occupying several strongholds were pushed north of the Danube. On his way back to Russia, Prince Svyatoslav was killed in an ambush by the Pechenegs. Northeastern Bulgaria fell to the Byzantines and Veliki Preslav was named after the victorious emperor.

All that had been achieved over the centuries fell into ruin in a short time and all hope seemed to have gone. At that point Bulgarian statehood was revived in the remote western areas. Nikola, a local count and rebel, had ruled them ever since the reign of Tsar Peter. Nikola's sons struggled fiercely against the Byzantines. The enemy was led by one of the most powerful emperors of all time, Basil II (976–1025), who was to be nicknamed Bulgaroctonus (Slayer of the Bulgarians).

Nikola had four sons, all of whom fell in battle except Samuil. Since Simeon's descendant, Tsar Boris II, died in an accident, the people unanimously proclaimed *Samuil Tsar* (976–1014). The Bulgarian capital moved temporarily to the Macedonian town of Ochrid and in the early 980s the Bulgarians laid waste the whole of Hellas.

In an attempt to strike back, the Emperor Basil II suffered a crushing defeat near Serdica (modern Sofia) on August 17, 986. In the next ten years Samuil reaped his greatest successes. He drove the Byzantines away from Northeastern Bulgaria and the old capital of Veliki Preslav. Having regained the north, the Bulgarian Tsar launched ravaging attacks against Byzantium, establishing his rule over the Adriatic coast, the whole of Macedonia and Northern Greece. In this victorious campaign Samuil suffered a single defeat in Central Greece in 996.

The Byzantines could not retaliate, being engaged in fierce battles with the Arabs to reconquer the whole of Syria. This gave Tsar Samuil an opportunity to concentrate on the northwest. First he punished the rebellious Serbian tribes and annexed their land after their Prince Chaslav died in 997. A quick war with the Hungarians ended in the annexation of the one-time Bulgarian areas along the middle reaches of the Danube, and a felicitous marriage of the Bulgarian heir to the throne to the daughter of Stephen, the first Hungarian King. It was at that time, however, that Basil II's difficulties in Asia Anterior ended.

In 1001 Basil II's huge armies headed for Northeastern Bulgaria where they took the same areas as in 971. The Byzantines conquered Tsar Samuil's main strongholds in the west slowly and methodically. The war turned into a series of sieges of the major towns Bdin (modern Vidin),Vereya, Skopje and Pernik. The Emperor pushed the Bulgarian tsar further and further westwards. Samuil's attempt to counter-attack near Thessalonica in 1009 ended in failure.

A Byzantine military campaign in Southern Italy unexpectedly gave the Bulgarians a brief respite. But in 1014

Basil II decided to end the long war of attrition. One of the biggest battles in history between Bulgarians and Byzantines took place on July 29, 1014. The Bulgarian army suffered a crushing defeat and 15,000 warriors were taken prisoner.

Nevertheless, Tsar Samuil made a last-ditch counter-attack and even scored some success. Then Basil II committed a brutality unprecedented even in the Middle Ages, which won him the nickname Bulgaroctonus (Slayer of the Bulgarians). He blinded the prisoners, leaving one one-eyed man in every hundred to lead his comrades to their tsar. Tsar Samuil had witnessed many wartime atrocities but the sight overpowered him and he died of a heart attack. His son *Gavrail Radomir* (1014–1015) succeeded to the throne.

The Bulgarian drama was entering its final act. Fierce fighting moved to the heart of the west, Macedonia. To make things worse, rivalry for the throne ended in murder. The Tsar was murdered by his first cousin *Ivan Vladislav* who was destined to be the last representative of the Samuil dynasty (1015–1018). Basil II stopped at nothing, razing Bulgarian towns and villages to the ground, killing and blinding men and women.

In the autumn of 1015 the Bulgarian military leader Ivats defeated part of the Byzantine troops and forced the Emperor to retreat temporarily. In 1017, however, Basil II launched a new campaign, which was also his last. He defeated Ivan Vladislav's army and in 1018 the BulgarianTsar was killed at the siege of a stronghold on the Adriatic coast.

Resistance seemed pointless, although the heir to the throne Persian and some of the military leaders insisted on fighting back. The Queen Mother Maria and Patriarch David decided to succumb to Byzantium. In March 1018 they presented an official letter to Basil II, ceding Bulgaria to its arch-enemy. The rulers of the biggest strongholds joined the memorandum. The heir to the throne and certain military leaders put up resistance from strongholds in the rugged mountains of Albania for some time. The last pockets of resistance were crushed at the turn of 1018.

Bulgaria lost its independence for more than 150 years.The attempt to follow an independent course in Orthodox culture, which had begun during the reign of Prince Boris-Mihail, was brought to an end by force. Thenceforth, the Bulgarians became part of the large family of the "Byzantine commonwealth of nations", as the British Byzantologist D. Obolenski aptly called the Orthodox community.

VI. BULGARIA IN THE BYZANTINE COMMONWEALTH

Year 1186 of the Christian Era. The Liberation

In the llth and 12th Centuries the Bulgarians shared the Byzantine Empire's successes and failures, of which there were quite a few. Basil II left a powerful state stretching from Italy and Central Europe to Mesopotamia and Syria. His successors, however, soon began to squander his legacy, indulging in amusements and court intrigue. Several decades of relative calm came to an abrupt end in 1071. The Byzantines suffered a total defeat from the Turks in the Battle of Manzikert in Asia Minor and their capital was threatened. Waves of Turkish tribes were to become the main problem of Byzantium and the Orthodox states in the Balkan Peninsula in the coming centuries.

More difficulties arose in the late llth and early 12th Centuries. The Normans attacked from the west via Sicily.They were seeking new places to settle and were conducting an aggressive policy across Europe. The Pechenegs, the Cumans and the Uzes, who belonged to the latest wave of the great people's migration, were flooding in from the east. The Balkan Peninsula was virtually overrun by them and was subjected to ravage and slaughter. At the very end of the llth Century the Crusaders appeared on the scene. Their incursions periodically laid waste the peninsula.

The strong dynasty of the Comneni ascended the Byzantine throne at this critical point. Its founder, Alexius I (1081–1118), repulsed the Normans and the northern barbarians. Not only did he make the passage of the First Crusade to Asia Minor painless for Byzantium, but he used the belligerent western knights to take Byzantine areas back from the Turks. His grandson, Manuel I Comnenus (1143–1180), nearly revived the Byzantines' dream of restoring the power and frontiers of the old Roman Empire.

Then, however, the weak dynasty of the Angeli succeeded to the throne. The Bulgarians had waited long for this moment. In fact, it was not their first attempt to take advantage of Byzantium's troubles in order to regain their independence. In 1040–1041 the western Bulgarian regions revolted against the social policy of one of Basil II's incompetent successors. The revolt grew into a popular uprising, headed by the sons of the last Bulgarian tsars, Peter Delyan and Alusian. Unfortunately, they rowed with one another just as their fathers had, which doomed the uprising to failure.

After the Byzantines were defeated at Manzikert, the Bulgarians rose again. In 1072–1073 Georgi Voitekh and Konstantin Bodin made an abortive attempt to restore the kingdom. More revolts, headed by Leka, Dobromir and Travul, took place in the last decades of the llth Century.

Those three rebels were Paulician and Bogomil heretics. The Bogomil heresy emerged in Bulgaria in the reign of Tsar Peter. Its followers were particularly antagonistic to the Byzantine authorities, or rather to any human authority. It was no coincidence that this Bulgarian heresy became widespread in Western Europe. It formed the basis for the teachings of the French Cathars and Albigenses, who caused a civil war between north and south in France.

Discontent among the Bulgarians persisted throughout the 12th Century. It peaked during the reign of Isaac II Angelus (1185–1195) who, like all rulers who lacked foresight, raised taxes first. At that very time two Bulgarian aristocrats, the brothers Asen and Peter, were insulted by the arrogant Byzantine administration. This sparked off an outburst of pent-up hatred, harboured for150 years.

A church built a short time before in the foothills of Turnovo, an impregnable stronghold in the Balkan Mountains, was consecrated in the cold autumn of 1186. The two brothers' estates lay nearby. The standard of revolt was raised along with the cross of the new church at the ceremony. The crowd proclaimed monk Vassily Archbishop. He, in turn, crowned *Peter Tsar* of the Bulgarians (1186–1190;1196–1197).

A harsh winter helped the organisers because the Byzantine punitive units could not cross the inaccessible passes of the Balkan Mountains. In the summer of 1187, however, the Byzantine Emperor launched an offensive against the rebels. He had no difficulty conquering areas north of the mountains, but the rebels hid in their fortresses, perched on top of rocky peaks, or crossed the Danube into a land unfamiliar to the Byzantines.

Energetic activity for the liberation of the Bulgarian lands started as soon as the Byzantines retreated. The rebels' fast-moving units acted jointly with the Cumans, a tribe of horsemen. This union was to prove very important in the coming decades. The allied army regained Northern Bulgaria in a short time and began to make daring inroads into the south. The uprising spread westwards at lightning speed, reaching as far as Macedonia.

The year 1188 was decisive for the uprising. This time Isaac II Angelus, an otherwise irresolute man, decided to put an end to the Bulgarian problem. He led a strong army through the passes of the Balkan Mountains and ravaged the north. The conflict was resolved at the strong fortress of Lovech, where the main forces of the rebels put up resistance for a full three months. The Emperor could not take the fortress and had to sign a peace treaty, by which he recognised de facto the Liberation of the Bulgarian state.

The Bulgarians had unexpected but much needed respite in 1189, when heavily armed German knights of the Third Crusade crossed Thrace, led by Frederick I Barbarossa. Shortly afterwards the Byzantine Emperor managed to organise a new campaign northwards and besieged Turnovo, which had already been proclaimed capital of the revived Bulgarian Kingdom.

Something in this battle strongly resembled the events of the early 9th Century. The inaccessible stronghold of Turnovo withstood the attack and the Byzantines began to retreat across the Balkan Mountains. A deadly ambush had been laid for them in one of the passes, which ended in a crushing defeat and carnage. Fleeing, the Emperor Isaac II Angelus had a narrow escape and never again thought of crossing the mountain. From then on military operations were conducted only in Thrace, the Aegean region and Macedonia. All efforts were concentrated on liberating all Bulgarian lands within the boundaries of the powerful 10th-Century Empire.

At that point Bulgaria was beset by internal dissension. In 1190 the elder brother, Peter, stepped down in favour of Asen who had made a name for himself as a remarkable military leader. *Tsar Asen I* (1190–1196) headed all victorious campaigns against Byzantium and the Hungarian Kingdom. The one-time Bulgarian regions of Belgrade and Branichevo on the middle reaches of the Danube regained their freedom in battle with the Hungarians.

Suddenly, Tsar Asen was murdered in 1196 by the treacherous hand of an aristocrat of his innermost circle. Peter had to take the reins of power again but he himself was killed by a plotter. Undoubtedly, the Byzantines were at the bottom of this villainy. They showed cunning and took advantage of the overweening ambitions and avarice of some of the new Bulgarian courtiers. Someone had to put the Bulgarian Kingdom in order. This was done by the third brother, Kaloyan, who had lived in the shadow of his elder brothers Asen and Peter until then.

Defeat of the French knights and Bulgaria's rise in the first half of the 13th Century

There are certain similarities between Kaloyan and Tsar Simeon the Great, who had lived 300 years earlier. Initially, they both seemed cut out for careers other than the throne, but eventually sat on it by force of circumstance. Both were sent to Constantinople as hostages where they were imbued with Byzantine culture. Much to the surprise of their contemporaries, however, these rulers struck terror into Bulgaria's enemies and won the greatest victories in its medieval history.

From the outset *Tsar Kaloyan* (1197–1207) subdued the unruly Bulgarian aristocrats with an iron hand. Alternating cruelty with diplomacy, he won back some breakaway administrators in Thrace and Macedonia. He also annexed more territories along the Black Sea coast and in Kossovo which had been part of the Bulgarian Kingdom.

Once state power had been restored, it was time to legitimise Bulgaria as part of the new European order. Like Prince Boris-Mihail before him, Tsar Kaloyan, too, played the Roman card. Conducting a brisk correspondence with Pope Innocent III (1198–1216), he achieved most of his goals. In the autumn of 1204 the title of King of the Bulgarians was bestowed on him and the Bulgarian spiritual leader received the title of Primas (Primate), which is a diplomatically modified version of the Orthodox rank of patriarch. In return, Kaloyan committed himself to introduce the Uniat, a hybrid between Catholicism and Orthodoxy. It should be noted that in his letters to the Pope the Bulgarian ruler referred to himself as Emperor, while remaining a Tsar to his own people.

At that point certain events shook the whole of Europe. In November 1199 at a knights' tournament in Champagne the most distinguished aristocrats of Northern France raised the cross and launched a new crusade for the liberation of the Holy Land. Many knights from all over France and Northern Italy soon joined them. The most blue-blooded nobles headed the Crusade: Baldwin IV, count of Flanders and Hainaut, Count Louis de Blois, Boniface of Montferrat, Thibaut, Count of Champagne and Brie. The Crusaders were joined by the Venetian Doge Enrico Dandolo who was to transport them on his ships.

All of a sudden the aim of the Fourth Crusade changed dramatically. Instead of fighting Muslims in the Holy Land, the French knights attacked Christians in the Byzantine Empire. Weakened by the recent internal conflicts, the Empire failed to put up strong resistance. After a short siege, the Crusaders took Constantinople in April 1204. The Latin Empire was established in place of Byzantium under Baldwin of Flanders and Hainaut, who became known as Baldwin I (1204–1205).

Forgetting their original plan, the Crusaders set about conquering territories of what had been the Eastern Roman Empire. Their forces advanced on Asia Minor, Greece and Thrace. It was only a matter of time before they clashed with the Bulgarian state. That is what happened before long. Tsar Kaloyan's peace offer met with a haughty, arrogant response from the French knights.

The decisive battle took place at Adrianople on April 14, 1205. The Bulgarians used certain stratagems to lure the Crusaders into an ingenious ambush. The subsequent carnage was terrible and merciless. Thousands of Crusaders and armour-bearers were killed or captured. A contemporary chronicler wrote that the flower of French chivalry perished at Adrianople. Most leaders of the Crusade were slain at the battle and the Emperor Baldwin I was captured and executed in Turnovo. The scale of the battle is comparable to the defeats of the Teutonic Knights at Lake Peipus (1242) and at Grunwald (1410).

But there was more trouble ahead for the Crusaders. In a series of battles at Seres and Arcadiopolis the French

knights suffered total defeats and their forces were deci-
mated. The new Latin Emperor of Constantinople Henry
(1206–1216) kept sending letters to the Pope and to France
asking for reinforcements, which arrived more and more
rarely. It had become clear that the Balkan Peninsula was
no place for armed Crusaders to roam.

Meanwhile, another leader of the Crusaders was killed:
Boniface of Montferrat, who had proclaimed himself King
of Thessalonica and a vassal of the Latin Emperor. Tsar
Kaloyan was an absolute ruler of Thrace and the Aegean
coast, while the Crusaders withdrew to Constantinople,Thessalonica and a few more towns they still held.
It seemed that the days of the Latin Empire were numbered.

Then, suddenly, rescue came. In the autumn of 1207 the
Bulgarian Tsar was preparing for the final assault on
Thessalonica when he was killed by a plotter in his tent
one night in October. A miracle happened: the Bulgarian
army withdrew into its own land and the Crusaders' Empire survived.

Tsar Boril (1207–1218) mounted the Bulgarian throne.
Being a relative of Kaloyan's, he had probably plotted the
coup himself. It was purely dynastic by nature and left
Bulgaria's attitude towards the Latin Empire unchanged.
However, the new tsar lacked Kaloyan's qualities and lost
important battles with the Crusaders, although he had a
military and a psychological advantage. Discontent with
his rule mounted, only to end in his deposition. Asen I's
son, *Ivan Asen II* (1218–1241), was proclaimed Tsar by
the aristocrats.

At that time the situation in the Balkan Peninsula was
radically different. Taking advantage of Tsar Kaloyan's
victories and the decline in the Crusaders' might, the
Byzantines began to revive their statehood in various
places in the former empire. Two centres became particularly strong: Epirus on the Adriatic coast and Nicaea in

Asia Minor. Initially, the former was the stronger of the two Byzantine states. Its ruler Theodore Comnenus did not conceal his ambitions to win back Constantinople and re-establish the Byzantine Empire.

It was with him that Tsar Ivan Asen II clashed. A battle with the Bulgarians stood between the Epirots and the realisation of their ambitions. The Byzantines suffered a total defeat at the Klokotnitsa Stream in Thrace on March 9, 1230. Within a short time Tsar Ivan Asen II conquered territories nearly as large as Simeon's state. Bulgaria bordered on the Adriatic, the Black Sea and the Aegean, and included the whole of Macedonia and Thrace. Through well-considered dynastic marriages the Bulgarian ruler obtained disputed areas around Belgrade and Branichevo from the Hungarians and then became a regent of the young heir to the throne of the Latin Empire.

Similarly to Tsar Kaloyan, Ivan Asen II skilfully used the religious differences between Orthodoxy and Catholicism. He achieved the restoration of the Bulgarian Orthodox Patriarchate by clever political moves in 1235. It was granted recognition at the ecumenical council in Lampsacus with the approval of all Orthodox patriarchs. Politically, it was achieved with the help of the Empire of Nicaea, which established itself as the only Byzantine successor state in that period.

It was in conjunction with the Nicaeans that the Bulgarian ruler launched a big campaign to seize Constantinople from the Latin Empire in 1237. Even though the siege failed, it provoked a strong reaction from the Catholic West. The Pope even called on the Western states to embark on a Crusade against the Eastern Christian heretics.

These negative consequences made Ivan Asen II reconsider his policy in the Balkan Peninsula. Towards the end of his life he sought closer relations with the Catholic states. This was prompted, inter alia, by the excessive strengthening of the Empire of Nicaea, which changed the status quo and weakened Bulgaria's position. It was not by mere chance that the Bulgarian ruler restored the state of Theodore Comnenus which he himself had destroyed. His aim was to make that satellite state a counterbalance to the rising power of the Nicaeans.

When Tsar Ivan Asen II died, the heirs to the throne were all minors. *Koloman*, his son by his first marriage to a Hungarian princess, was tsar until 1246, when he was succeeded, until 1256, by *Mihail II Asen*, his son by his Byzantine wife Irina. In both cases power was in the hands of regents appointed by the stronger political parties of the Turnovo court. There were fierce struggles between separate cliques, which often ended in assassination. This destabilised the state. In a short time Bulgaria lost large areas in Thrace, Macedonia and the Rhodope Mountains. Finally, a civil war broke out over the succession in 1256. It was triggered off by the death of Tsar Mihail II Asen, who was killed in a conspiracy. A one-year struggle over the succession was won by the prominent aristocrat *Konstantin Tikh*, who reigned from 1257 to 1277. This broke the direct line of succession to the throne of the Asen dynasty.

Meanwhile, important events took place in the Balkan Peninsula. In 1261 the Nicaeans won back Constantinople and restored the Byzantine Empire under the Palaeologi.The Latin Empire became a thing of the past, although its remnants survived until the 14th Century. This is how the French knights' attempt to found a large state in Southeastern Europe ended. A new, terrible threat was looming over the Balkan Peninsula, one which had already plagued large parts of Europe: the Tartar hordes.

The Terter dynasty and the Tartar invasion

Social tension had been mounting for decades when it exploded with fearful might at the end of the reign of Konstantin Tikh. Having overrun the Russian principalities and other northern peoples, the Tartars' powerful Golden Horde became a neighbour of the Bulgarian state. It made systematic incursions and pillaged areas south of the Danube. Byzantium and Hungary also took every opportunity to attack the weakened Bulgarian Kingdom. As is usual in history, political and economic difficulties made the plight of the common people worse.

In 1277 they ran out of patience. Somewhere in Northeastern Bulgaria a peasant named Ivailo spread the word that he had been sent by God to help the poor. Thus the greatest anti-feudal peasant revolt in the Balkan Peninsula began in a typically medieval manner. Hopeful poor people rallied round the self-styled messiah and formed armed units.

The human masses first confronted the Tartar looters. In several successive battles the invaders were defeated and driven north of the Danube. Afterwards the peasant crowds headed for the capital Turnovo to punish those whom they unanimously considered incompetent rulers and who were to blame for all hardships. The Tsar's army tried to stop them but was swept away and Konstantin Tikh was killed.

After a short siege the rebels entered the capital. *Ivailo* agreed to marry the queen dowager and was proclaimed Tsar (1278–1280). This proclamation of a "peasant tsar" is a rare example of the dream of all medieval anti-feudal uprisings coming true. Throughout his reign, however, Ivailo had to counter internal and external blows. The Byzantines did not fail to interfere and nominated their own claimant to the throne of the Asen dynasty. After a series of victories and defeats, the peasant Tsar Ivailo had to seek refuge in the land of the enemies, the Tartars, where he was killed.

Meanwhile, the Bulgarian aristocracy closed ranks in the face of popular unrest and external intervention. The state was in a shambles because, despite good intentions, popular revolts tend to leave a country in disarray and economic chaos. A daring and experienced ruler was needed to mount the throne. The aristocrats proclaimed *Georgi I Terter* (1280–1292) Tsar. He was of the well known aristocratic family of the Terters.

The reign of this dynasty has been ambivalently assessed. On the one hand, it strengthened the Tsar's power. On the other hand, the Terters had neither the authority nor the talent of the Asen dynasty. Georgi I Terter tried to pursue an active policy towards the Catholic states, Byzantium and Serbia. However, the Tartar threat always loomed large over him until he became an immediate vassal of Khan Nogai. The Bulgarian ruler had to let the Tartars hold his son hostage and in 1292 he abdicated and took monastic vows.

Bickering among the aristocrats and foreign policy intrigues brought *Tsar Smilets* (1292–1298) to the throne. His reign was marked by dismemberment of the kingdom by feudal lords, as a result of which several regions, including Vidin and Krun, broke away to become semi-independent. Separating from the mother country, they fell easy prey to their neighbours: Byzantines, Serbs, Hungarians and Tartars.

Smilets died leaving Bulgäria without a ruler, which led to one of the most disgraceful episodes in its history. Khan Nogai's son Chaka occupied the throne in 1299. From a historical perspective, however, this episode can be seen as a clever move by *Teodor Svetoslav*, Georgi I Terter's son, who was held hostage by the Tartars. He himself brought Chaka to Turnovo and shortly afterwards plotted against the Tartar and killed him. Then the Bulgarian aristocrats readily and unanimously proclaimed him tsar (1300–1322).

The new tsar's main achievement was the elimination of the Tartar threat. Teodor Svetoslav shrewdly took advantage of dissension in the Golden Horde. Killing Chaka, he played in favour of the claimant Toktu, who became khan before long. To show his gratitude, the Tartar ruler returned to Bulgaria the lands in the north and freed them from vassalage. The tsar unobtrusively cleared the capital of the Tartars' supporters, who had become numerous during the troubled times.

Bulgaria began to conduct an active policy for the first time in fifty years. To start with, Teodor Svetoslav re-established state power in the semi-independent regions. Recapturing the Krun region was particularly important since it separated the Bulgarian state from Byzantium.Using this territory as a base, Tsar Teodor Svetoslav attacked the Byzantines in the battle of Skafida in 1304.They suffered a crushing defeat, which was followed by the signing of a peace treaty in 1308.

A civil war broke out in Byzantium in 1321. It was Bulgaria's turn to interfere in the internal affairs of its southern neighbour. Teodor Svetoslav was quick to do so in alliance with the Serbs. At the height of the preparations he died, but his son *Georgi II Terter* carried on his mission and conquered the Plovdiv region. Suddenly in 1322 the new Tsar died, too, in unclear circumstances during a campaign against the Byzantines.

The death of the Bulgarian Tsar was followed by renewed dynastic feuds, only this time they ended quickly and painlessly. *Mihail III Shishman* (1323–1330) was proclaimed Tsar in Turnovo. This strengthened the position of the state because he was a hereditary ruler of the Vidin region, which was quite independent from central power.The Shishman dynasty ascended the throne. It was to rule during the last decades of independent medieval Bulgaria.

Tsar Ivan Alexander (1331–1371) and the Second Golden Age of medieval Bulgaria

The civil war in Byzantium lasted for eight years. Throughout that time Tsar Mihail III Shishman took every opportunity to derive benefits for Bulgaria from the internecine war and his army nearly entered Constantinople at one point. As the Emperor Andronicus III Palaeologus (1329–1341) mounted the throne, the war was brought to an end and in 1329 the two states signed a peace treaty. It was openly directed against Serbia, which had benefited most from the general weakening of its neighbours.

In the 13th Century the obscure Serbian state gradually expanded. In 1217 it was proclaimed a kingdom, and under King Stephen Milutin seized a large portion of Macedonia. Taking advantage of Bulgaria's and Byzantium's difficulties, the Serbs penetrated into the south. This led to the events of 1329–1330.

The plan was to eliminate Serbian domination over Macedonia, with the Bulgarians attacking from the east and the Byzantines from the south. Being too self-assertive, Mihail III Shishman did not wait for all his troops to rally and headed for the Serbian border. The decisive battle took place at Velbuzhd (modern Kyustendil) on July 28, 1330. The Bulgarians were defeated and their severely wounded Tsar died after a few days. Serbia's road to Macedonia was clear. Disputes over the succession caused confusion in the capital Turnovo. The Serbs, of all people, tried to interfere in choosing the new ruler, but in 1331 the problem was resolved by installing as *Tsar Ivan Alexander*, ruler of the big town of Lovech and cousin of the slain Tsar. The succession of the Shishman dynasty was continued in a collateral line. Tsar Ivan Alexander took control of foreign policy as early as 1331–1332. He defeated the Byzantines in a surprise attack at Rusokastro in Eastern

Thrace, thus pre-empting a strike they might have attempted after Bulgaria's unexpected debacle at Velbuzhd. Problems with Serbia were ironed out as the powerful King Stephen Dushan married Ivan Alexander's sister Elena. The Bulgarian ruler subdued the unruly aristocrats and ensured a lasting peace for the state.

A new civil war broke out in Byzantium in 1341. Tsar Ivan Alexander took advantage and conquered disputed lands in the Rhodope Mountains and Thrace in a bloodless campaign. There were more conflicts with the Byzantines over Black Sea towns in the 1360s. In 1366 the Byzantines ordered the fleet of the sixth Count Amadeus of Savoy to attack the Bulgarian towns on the Black Sea coast. The ironclad knights and their artillery took some of the Black Sea strongholds in the south for the Byzantines.

Wars were waged with the Hungarian Kingdom as well but, on the whole, the long reign of Tsar Ivan Alexander was peaceful. This made it possible for Bulgarian medieval culture to reach new heights, known as the Second Golden Age. Of course, this progress was a result of the overall development of the Bulgarian state between the 12th and 14th Centuries.

Bulgaria's steady integration into the "Byzantine Commonwealth of peoples" influenced all spheres of life. Although they were Orthodox Christians, in the 9th and 10th Centuries the Bulgarians tried to distance themselves from contemporary Byzantine culture and followed models of Early Christian civilisation in architecture, painting, writing, and so on.

Architectural monuments were completely uniform between the 12th and 14th Centuries. Bulgarians, Byzantines and Serbs built similar fortresses in the same fashion. They chose steep, naturally protected slopes. A citadel was built at the top to be used as a last refuge by the inhabitants. The town proper, also surrounded by stone walls, developed around it. Districts and suburbs emerged in larger populated centres and were included in the general fortification structures at a certain stage. Thousands of fortresses were built in the mountain ranges for the purpose of defending passes. They played an important role in the defence of the strongly centralised Eastern Orthodox states and were controlled by the respective rulers. They often changed their rulers in the course of internal conflicts and wars, but never turned into Western-style castles, which were the strongholds of petty feudal lords.

Church construction was a priority as in earlier epochs. Imposing basilicas, in which a multitude of people could gather, were a thing of the distant past. The Orthodox Christians who lived between the 12th and 14th Centuries liked small, compact, domed churches shaped like the symbol of their faith, the cross. They were lavishly decorated with rows of blind arcades, small columns, bricks and decorative clay saucers. Such masterpieces have been preserved in the rich medieval towns of Nessebur, Cheren, Turnovo and Melnik.

Paintings are the central feature of the Orthodox church. Magnificent 13th Century frescoes have been preserved in *the Forty Holy Martyrs Church* in Turnovo and *the Boyana Church* near Sofia. In the 14th Century Bulgarian art joined the mainstream, called by modern scholars "the style of the Palaeologi". The surviving Bulgarian monuments are among the finest examples of Byzantine art in its final stage. Some of the classic examples are the murals in the rock churches of Ivanovo, the chapel of Hrelyo's Tower at Rila Monastery, and the church at Zemen Monastery.

Fourteenth Century painting illustrates the heated ideological disputes which characterised the public life of the Christian states in the Balkan Peninsula. They originated in Constantinople and gained currency in Bulgaria during the reign of Tsar Ivan Alexander. The Bulgarian Tsar organised and himself attended several church councils which condemned various heresies.

The greatest number of manuscripts have survived from the time of Ivan Alexander, who personally commissioned many of them. These works are accompanied by author's notes describing the Bulgarian ruler as an enlightened book-lover, similar to Tsar Simeon the Great. The most ornately illuminated Bulgarian manuscripts preserved from the Middle Ages date from the reign of Ivan Alexander. They are among the masterpieces exhibited at the most famous museums of the world: a copy of the *Manasses Chronicle* (1344–1345) in the Vatican, the *Tetraevangelium* (1355–1356), also known as the Gospel of Tsar Ivan Alexander, in the British Museum, London, the *Tomich Psalter* (1360) in the Moscow State Museum, to mention only a few.

Books written at the time of Tsar Ivan Alexander covered various subjects, from religion and theosophy to history. They represent the wide spectrum of interests and concerns of 14th-Century Bulgarian society. They were made in scriptoriums which were schools and libraries all in one. There is evidence suggesting that the proportion of educated people at the time was quite substantial. This extensive knowledge was not confined to Bulgaria. A literary reform carried out by the great man of letters, Patriarch Euthymius, in the third quarter of the 14th Century left its mark on the entire literature of the Orthodox Slavs. This process is known in modern science as the second Bulgarian cultural influence. From Bulgaria, books spread to Serbia, Wallachia, Moldova and Russia. The southern Slavic influence on Russia was particularly strong. Its literature and spiritual life as a whole was formed under that influence for centuries ahead.

VII. THE DARK AGES
OF OTTOMAN RULE

Year 1395 of the Christian Era. The drama

In the second half of the 13th Century there was a small Turkish principality in the middle of Asia Minor. It was headed by the combative Emir Osman, who was always fighting the neighbouring Turkish rulers and the Byzantines to the west. The latter did not pay much attention to him until 1302 when they were defeated twice and lost nearly all their lands in Asia Minor within a few months. This was the early history of what was to become the Ottoman Empire.

Over the next few decades the Turks strengthened their position and in 1354 they settled in the Balkan Peninsula. Their advance was amazing, but the rulers of the Christian states inexplicably turned a blind eye to the danger. It was not until 1370-1371 that an anti-Turkish coalition began to form. However, Sultan Murad I (1362–1389) launched pre-emptive strikes. He first defeated the Byzantines and took Adrianople, and then routed the Serbian army at the Maritza River on September 26, 1371. Left on their own, the Bulgarians had to brace themselves to resist the invasion.

That year the elderly Tsar Ivan Alexander died and *Ivan Shishman* (1371–1395) was enthroned. He was a child of the Bulgarian ruler's romantic relationship with a Jewish woman. In 1348 the Tsar divorced his wife Teodora and married Sarah, who was baptised and adopted the same Christian name. It was bad for the state, however, that Ivan Alexander deprived his only surviving son by his first marriage, Ivan Sratsimir, of the right to succeed to the throne. By way of compensation, he sent him to Vidin, the hereditary town of the Shishman family, and let him style himself tsar. Nevertheless, this move of Ivan Alexander's led to contention which would to some extent be fatal for the Bulgarian state.

Tsar Ivan Shishman had to face the formidable Turkish army a few months after he mounted the throne. Having defeated the Serbs at the Maritza, the Turks immediately headed for the large Bulgarian town of Sredets (modern Sofia). They were stopped by the rather small army of the Tsar's younger son Ivan Asen, named after the illustrious Asen brothers, who were close relatives of the Shishman family. After a few brief engagements, the Bulgarians fought a big battle near modern Sofia. The invaders were driven away southwards but Ivan Asen was slain. His sacrifice gave the Bulgarians a respite of several years before the decisive clash.

This victory, in which royal blood was shed, allowed Tsar Ivan Shishman to defy a Turkish ultimatum that his sister Tamara become the Sultan's wife. Later on, however, the Tsar had to comply, as well as to become a Turkish vassal. As to territorial losses, in 1371 Bulgaria lost lands south of the Balkan Mountains. However, there were no incursions into the north, except for the seizure of Sredets in 1382. The town had been under siege for ten years and was finally taken by deception.

Meanwhile, the Turks were strengthening their position in the Balkan Peninsula and expanding their territory. They occupied the whole of Thrace and most of Macedonia. The once powerful Byzantine Empire was reduced to the immediate vicinity of Constantinople and the Peleponnes. Sultan Murad I was getting ready for a decisive encounter with the Bulgarians and the Serbs. A pretext was found in 1387 when Ivan Shishman, whose power had grown, refused to meet his obligations as a vassal. The next year the Grand Vizier Ali Pasha and all prominent Turkish military leaders retaliated by leading a huge army against Tsar Ivan Shishman. Sultan Murad I had made himself clear: they were to crush the infidels and destroy the Bulgarian state.

The Ottoman hordes crossed the Balkan Mountains in the autumn of 1388. Using deception and pretending to have peaceful intentions, the invaders made their way into several fortresses, including the key ones, Shoumen and Madara. The Bulgarian garrisons soon realised what the real purpose of the campaign was. They put up stronger resistance and the conquerors showed who they were: the laws of the "jihad, the holy war in the name of Islam", were enforced. This meant that strongholds which put up resistance were razed to the ground and their defenders were massacred. This fate befell the town of Venchan which dared to resist the Turks.

And yet the Bulgarians withstood the attack. The invaders were stopped, with Shoumen their only conquest north of the Balkan Mountains. Another reason for their withdrawal was that they had problems on other fronts. In 1389 Sultan Murad I clashed with the allied forces of the Serbs. He was killed at the famous battle of Kossovo Plain but the Turks won a decisive victory. Sultan Bayezid I (1389–1402), nicknamed Lightning, skilfully enhanced the victory, establishing a lasting presence in the western part of the peninsula and crossing the Danube into Wallachia.

Soon afterwards he had to return to Asia Minor for a while to put down a riot. Tsar Ivan Shishman took the opportunity to recapture Shoumen and launched an offensive southwards in alliance with other Christian rulers. However, he had underestimated the strength of his dangerous enemy. In 1393 Sultan Bayezid I coped with the unrest and organised a large campaign against Bulgaria with the intention to teach the disobedient vassal a lesson once and for all.

A heroic and tragic struggle ensued. The numerically inferior Bulgarian army defended every fortress and tower. Chronicles tell the story of the dramatic sieges of Kossovo, Cherven and Svishtov. Turnovo fell after a siege lasting several weeks. At that time Tsar Ivan Shishman was not in the town and the defence was conducted by the spiritual leader of the people, Patriarch Euthymius. Once the Bulgarian capital was taken, the ruthless invaders put to the sword the captured aristocrats and warriors.

Pressed on from all sides, Tsar Ivan Shishman fought back from the town of Nikopolis (modern Nikopol), a strong fortress on the Danube. The Turkish siege was unsuccessful and the rump Bulgarian state survived for some time. Ivan Shishman did not stop fighting during those infinitely hard years. He made unflagging efforts to act in alliance with other independent Christian rulers in the region, mainly those of Wallachia and the Hungarian Kingdom. Recently found documents show that the Bulgarian Tsar hectically tried to rally the remnants of his defeated army, sending circular letters to surviving military leaders.

The showdown came in 1395. Sultan Bayezid I led his army north of the Danube against the Wallachian Prince Mircea. A fearful battle was fought on May 17, in which large numbers of Christians and Muslims lost their lives. Neither side won a decisive victory, but the Turks had to retreat.

It has become known with certainty only recently that the indefatigable Ivan Shishman himself took part in the monumental battle. He was captured by the Sultan's men on his way back to Nikopolis. Soon afterwards the Turks executed the great Tsar and seized the last remaining Bulgarian towns. That is how the conquest of the Turnovo kingdom ended.

Ivan Shishman's sons had a bizarre fate. Alexander, the successor to the throne, succumbed to the Turks and accepted Islam, although he had valiantly fought against them previously. In return for his defection he was made administrator of a large area in Asia Minor. His younger brother Fruzhin, however, emigrated to Hungary and continued the struggle.

First attempts at liberation (15th–17th Centuries)

Ivan Shishman was dead but the Bulgarians' hopes were still alive and were pinned on *Tsar Ivan Sratsimir* of Vidin. Until then he had stood aside from the bloody wars but, eventually, his small region turned out to be the last remaining independent Bulgarian territory. In 1396 an opportunity opened up for Ivan Sratsimir not only to keep it, but even to liberate the whole Bulgarian kingdom.

That year the Hungarian King and German Emperor Sigismund organised an impressive crusade against the Turks, which was backed by the Vatican and many European states. A great number of French, German and Hungarian knights joined the colours. Ivan Sratsimir lost no time in sending his forces to support the Crusaders,whose army was heading for the important stronghold of Nikopolis, at that time a major Turkish fortress. There, on September 25, 1396, the Western knights suffered total defeat in a horrible battle. Ivan Sratsimir was captured and the northwestern Bulgarian lands around Vidin were incorporated into the Ottoman Empire.

This is how five dark centuries of Ottoman domination over Bulgaria began. It was not uniformly oppressive throughout that period. At first the conquerors let the subjugated peoples enjoy considerable freedoms. Registers of that time show that many Christian feudal lords retained their privileges. In that period the Empire's riches came mainly from the new territories rather than from exploitation of its internal resources.

However, in the 16th and 17th Centuries the strength of the Ottoman Empire began to decline. The Turks lost important battles and wars against Iran, Austria and Venice. The huge state was disintegrating slowly but surely. Those were the worst years for the Christians in the Empire, who became victims of cruel religious persecution and economic oppression.

It was very difficult, not to say impossible, to put up resistance in the centralised Turkish state. The Muslim faith, alien and hostile, set Turks against Bulgarians, on which the imperial government capitalised. It insidiously taught poor Turks that they were superior to the Christians. Thus the ancient Roman principle "Divide and rule" was applied successfully.

The Bulgarians were barred from professing their religion, or were forced to do so out of sight of "the true believers", the Turks. They were forced to build low dome-less churches, sunk below ground level. The opulent Orthodox church rituals were banned. Massive Turkicisation in the 16th and 17th Centuries changed the demographic characteristics of entire Bulgarian regions. Members of the same family often professed different religions, lived in different villages and deeply loathed one another.

And yet the Bulgarians started to put up resistance from the very first years of Ottoman rule. More often than not it was unorganised and grassroots popular movement. Peasants opposed the Turkish authorities by refusing to pay the numerous taxes or fulfil various obligations. They deserted from the auxiliary military units of the Turkish army in which Christians were usually enlisted.

Such acts were followed by reprisals by the Turkish authorities. The need for self-defence led to the formation of many units which roamed the uninviting Bulgarian mountains and punished the oppressors. The official authorities outlawed them as bandits, but in most cases they were actually avengers and defenders of the people. Thus the interests of the conquerors and the underprivileged Christian population were balanced to some extent at grassroots level.

The anti-Turkish uprisings which broke out as early as the 15th Century marked the culmination of resistance. In 1408 a massive uprising broke out in the western territories and scared the oppressors. Putting their fathers' feud behind them, Fruzhin and Konstantin, sons of the last tsars Ivan Shishman and Ivan Sratsimir, headed the revolt. They had emigrated to Hungary where the King received them well and gave them land. The two cousins did not forget their country, however, and returned there to head the popular uprising. The uprising failed but nevertheless, it showed the Turks that the Bulgarians had not passively put up with bondage.

The Bulgarians were buoyed again with new hope for liberation in 1443–1444 when the Polish King Wladislaw III Jagiello and the Transylvanian Prince John Hunyadi organised a big Polish-Hungarian Crusade against the Turkish scourge. The allied Christian armies made two deep thrusts into the territory of the Empire. In 1444 they crossed the whole of Northern Bulgaria, defeating the Muslims and taking all their fortresses. The decisive battle of Varna involved Christians from Central and Southeastern Europe, including many Bulgarian detachments. The Turks won an overwhelming victory and the Polish King was killed.

Understandably, one of the main centres of resistance was the old capital Turnovo, populated by proud-spirited people and remnants of the old aristocracy. In 1592-1606 the European states formed a new coalition against Turkey which was already showing signs of decline. The Bulgarians' hopes for freedom were boosted particularly by the incursions of the mighty Wallachian Prince Michael the Brave, whose frequent assaults south of the Danube nourished their faith.

In 1598 a notable from Nikopol, Teodor Balm, a descendant of the old Turnovo aristocracy, devised a bold plot. He left for the old capital together with envoys of the Austrian Emperor. There Teodor Balin and Metropolitan Dionysy organised an uprising of the local notables with the single aim of reestablishing the kingdom. There is evidence that Teodor Balin was a rich man, respected by the Turkish authorities. The uprising was put down and he lost everything, but he had done all he could for his oppressed homeland.

The second Turnovo uprising broke out in 1686 in similar circumstances. The aggression of the Ottoman Empire across Europe was checked resolutely for the first time and the Christians were on the offensive on all fronts. The Holy Alliance consisted of Austria, Poland and Venice, later joined by Russia. The Turnovo uprising was provoked by the victories of the Alliance and sought to restore the Bulgarian monarchy. The rebels proclaimed tsar one Rostislav Sratsimirovich, believed to be a successor to the Bulgarian rulers. This uprising was quelled, too. It was the last attempt of the old aristocracy to regain Bulgaria's independence.

More and more uprisings were headed by representatives of the newly rich Third Estate: merchants, artisans and well-to-do peasants. During the same big war between Turkey and the Holy Alliance a massive uprising broke out in the ore-mining town of Chiprovtsi (Northwestern Bulgaria) in 1688. Its leaders were G.Peyachevich and I. Stanislavov. A year later the unrest spread into Macedonia where it was headed by Karposh.The rebels' hopes were shattered, however. The Austrian troops advancing on the Balkan Peninsula soon withdrew and the oppressed Christians were left without support.The Turkish authorities took advantage and retaliated with fire and sword across the rebel territories.

Though unsuccessful, the early uprisings in the Ottoman Empire manifested the Bulgarians' resolve to fight for freedom. Europe was embarking upon the Modern Age which ruled out the Turks' archaic cruel practices. Meanwhile the Bulgarian population was mustering courage for a decisive encounter with the conquerors.

Orthodox culture: a pillar of Bulgarian national consciousness

The Turkish invasion of the Balkan Peninsula left a deep imprint on all spheres of Christian life, its effect on culture being particularly strong. The Byzantine Orthodox civilisation was a sophisticated, complex system which could develop normally only if the state protected it. Stripped of its protection and stifled by a hostile religion, the culture was doomed to decline and extinction. But before it perished, the Byzantine cultural model played one final role, protecting the Orthodox Christians from assimilation and moral degradation. A parallel could be drawn with the high civilisations of Central America which were destroyed by a culture which, notwithstanding its technological and military superiority, was morally and intellectually inferior: the culture of the Spanish Conquistadors.

It has already been mentioned that the 14th Century marked the highest point of Bulgarian medieval literature. At the end of the century Bulgaria, engulfed in the fire of the invasion, had nearly flickered out. The most educated Bulgarians emigrated. The prominent writer Konstantin of Kostenets was a major literary figure at the Serbian court in the first half of the 15th Century, where he was known as the Philosopher. Patriarch Euthymius's disciples Grigory Tsamblak and Kiprian left for Russia. They spread Bulgarian literature in the vast country of the northern Orthodox Christians. For decades they were the heads and organisers of the Russian Church and became Muskovite metropolitans.

Monasteries in Serbia, Wallachia, Moldova and Russia were filled with Bulgarian men of letters teaching their Christian Orthodox brothers. The comparatively lenient attitude of the Turkish authorities in the 15th Century provided an opportunity for many of them to stay in the Bulgarian lands. At that time Vladislav the Grammarian and

Dimiter Cantacuzene worked in Macedonia and at Rila Monastery. A major historical work by an unknown writer dates from that period. It marked the beginning of a trend in Wallachian historiography.

In the 16th Century the attitude of the Turkish authorities towards the Bulgarians began to harden. Stakes and gallows appeared in the squares where martyrs died for the Christian faith, refusing to accept Islam. Two such men were Georgi, a goldsmith, and Nikola, a shoemaker, both from Sofia. The Church canonised them and writers described their sufferings. Those writers were Priest Peyo and Matei the Grammarian, who had gained prominence among their contemporaries and were patrons of culture known in the western parts of the country.

Despite the hardships caused by Ottoman rule, the Bulgarians needed simpler literature to read after their daily toil. Various stories, lives and edifying reading appeared in collections known as Damascenes, most of them translated from Greek. They became most widespread in the 17th and 18th Centuries. The Rila monk Yossif the Bearded was a very active compiler and translator of such writings.

The new age brought in printing. Since there was no ground to develop it in the Ottoman Empire, the first Bulgarian printed books were published abroad. In the 16th Century Bozhidar Vukovich and Yakov Kraikov had collections of writings in Bulgarian printed in Venice. In 1651 Filip Stanislavov's *Abagar* was published in Rome. In 1714 the first Bulgarian secular book, Hristofor Zhefarovich's *Stemmatigraphion*, was printed in Vienna. It was a translation but it is the author's comments that are valuable to Bulgarians.

The conquerors had destroyed most Bulgarian fortresses during the invasion. Initially, the building of new strongholds in the interior of the country where the Bulgarian lands lay was not part of their aggressive policy. When this became necessary in the 16th and 17th Centuries, artillery was by now in use, which necessitated different models of fortification. Lonely dilapidated towers stood perched here and there on steep peaks as reminders of the past glory of the Bulgarian Kingdom.

The local people were driven away to mountainous and semi-mountainous regions, while the invaders settled in the fertile plains. It is there that some architectural monuments have survived, which illustrate the lifestyle of well-to-do Bulgarians from the 15th to the 18th Centuries. They are mostly imposing stone towers of several storeys which served as dwellings and afforded protection in times of trouble. Such homes have been preserved inVratsa and Kratovo (now in the Former Yugoslav Republic of Macedonia). The large population centre of Arbanassi near Veliko Turnovo features some particularly impressive houses of rich families. Built as big as palaces, with dozens of rooms and banqueting halls, they were also designed to withstand the enemy's assaults. These structures represent the way of life of a small part of the Christian population in the Ottoman Empire, who had gained and enjoyed certain privileges. Later on the situation in the state slowly began to normalise and the Bulgarians grew richer and re-settled in the plains. Their homes began to look less like fortresses, while it was the beauty of their interior and exterior that mattered increasingly.

The village of Arbanassi has some of the most beautiful and imposing churches in the Bulgarian land from that period. They are huge buildings decorated with beautiful frescoes. The Turks ignored them because the local notables were among the richest merchants and stock-breeders in the Empire. Elsewhere, however, the ban on building high churches with domes and belfries stayed in force until the 19th Century. The Bulgarians were allowed to build imposing churches only in secluded monasteries. Such churches were built at the Poganovo, Bachkovo and Rila monasteries in the early centuries of Ottoman rule.

The Christian churches still combined architecture and paintings but the earlier heights were reached less frequently because of the existing bans and the general decline in art. In a matter of years after Bulgaria was conquered, a second layer of murals was painted at *the SS Peter and Paul Church* in Turnovo. They are in the style of 14th Century high painting, the saints' gloomy furrowed faces and long wildly waving beards and clothes conveying the horror and hopelessness gripping the Bulgarians.

The second half of the 15th Century is represented by a few surviving ensembles of paintings in the old tradition.Those are the frescoes in the churches of the Dragalevtsi Monastery (1476) and the Kremikovtsi Monastery (1493), both near Sofia, and the Poganovo Monastery (1499).The frescoes were commissioned by influential Bulgarian aristocrats whose likenesses were painted in the churches, such as Radoslav the Moor and Radivoi.

There is ample evidence that when the Turks' hostility against the Christians grew in severity during the16th and 17th Centuries, the former liquidated the old Bulgarian aristocracy first. Quite a few small churches have survived from that time, but none of the frescoes in them were commissioned by a well-known aristocrat. All donors were rich merchants, artisans and stock-breeders.

Thus the Bulgarian people approached its National Revival, albeit with some delay due to circumstances. The new culture was steadily departing from the principles of Byzantine civilisation and was eager to adopt the ideas of modern Western society. Like any extinct civilisation, Byzantine civilisation left its mark on the Christian peoples, but the future was to be governed by its own laws.

VIII. BULGARIAN REVIVAL (1700–1878)

After the Ottoman conquest of the Bulgarian state in1396, its natural development was abruptly halted by a power totally alien to the Christian tradition. The Bulgarian Revival, which began in the 18th Century, was the beginning of a return to the values of European civilisation. It was a time of transition from the closed medieval life to the modern era of economic recovery, cultural change and political activism.

The Ottoman Empire at a crossroads

Yet another war between the Ottoman Empire and its European enemies ended unexpectedly badly for the Empire in 1699, which sustained its first serious territorial losses. It became obvious by 1700 that the powerful Islamic presence in Europe was already a thing of the past due to the deep crisis in which the Empire of the Grand Turk had been plunged. The reformist attempts of some of the more far-sighted sultans met with the extreme conservatism of the Ulema (the class of Muslim doctors of sacred law and theology), the Sufi (the Islamic mystics) and the corrupt bureaucracy. Throughout the 18th and19th Centuries the Ottoman Empire was torn by the necessity to map its strategic path of development, choosing between the conservative Islamic tradition and European modernism.

This conflict surfaced in an interesting way at the very beginning of the 18th Century. Sultan Ahmed III (1703–1730) took the helm of the empire. He was an educated studious man, whose major shortcoming was the complete lack of interest in the management of state affairs. In the first fifteen years of his rule he changed about a dozen grand viziers. One of them, Ibrahim Pasha, gave impetus to the attempt to carry out reform. A proponent of Eastern methods and European ideas, Ibrahim took a series of measures intended to strengthen the Empire. He tried to improve the shaky financial system and curb the devaluation of the local currency, proposed changes in the military system, tried to put the judiciary under control and even opened the first Ottoman printing house. The time of Ahmed III and Ibrahim was a period of unprecedented adoption of European manners: the Ottoman court was fascinated by the French court ceremonial, new palaces were built as replicas of Versailles, masked balls, night sailings in the Bosphorus and firework displays were organised. The craze of the time was the cultivation of Dutch tulips, of which hundreds of thousands were imported. Predictably, Islamic reactionaries and those affected by the attempted reforms pooled their efforts against the reformist vizier. They attacked serious reforms – claiming, for instance, that the printing press came from the non-believers and must not print the texts of the Koran, as well as European fashions, which were offensive to the fanatic's eye. A revolt broke out and Ahmed III was forced to kill the reformist vizier. The only trace left from the failed attempt at Europeanisation was the name of this period of Turkish history, known as the "tulip period".

The return to the straight path did nothing to improve the situation of the Empire. Its traditional enemies Austria, Spain and Venice were joined by another fearsome foe, Russia. From Peter the Great onwards, all Russian emperors had been devising plans to expand southwards and drive the Turks away from the Black Sea and the Straits (the Bosphorus and the Dardanelles). Catherine the Great (1762– 1796) was very successful in this respect: she gained an outlet to the Black Sea and forced Turkey to sign a humiliating treaty in 1774, making many concessions to Russia. The war which led to that treaty had another important effect: military operations were transferred to the Balkan Pen-

The frescoes at Boyana Church were painted by masters of the Turnovo school of painting. Breaking with the official Byzantine canon, they portrayed people infused with the ancient ideal of beauty. Sebastocratress Dessislava: fresco, Boyana Church near Sofia (1259)

Tsar Ivan Alexander (1331-1371) and his wife Theodora with their sons Ivan Asen and Ivan Shishman: a miniature from the most lavishly and exquisitely illuminated medieval Bulgarian manu-script. It contains 366 miniatures and was given as a gift to trav-eller Robert Curzon by St Paul's Monastery on Mount Athos

A Gospel cover of gold-plated silver repousse and enamel

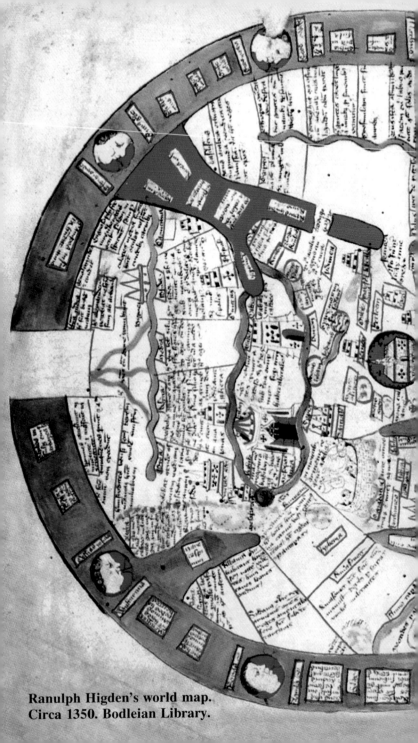

**Ranulph Higden's world map.
Circa 1350. Bodleian Library.**

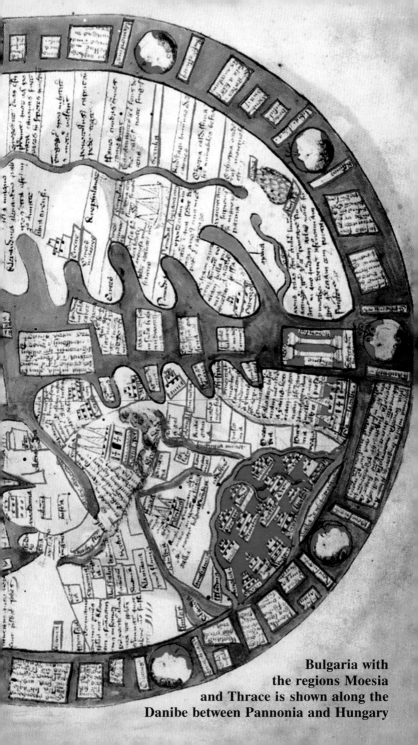

Bulgaria with
the regions Moesia
and Thrace is shown along the
Danibe between Pannonia and Hungary

МР ΘΥ ΙC   ΙC ΧC   ΔΙΣ

ΕΓΩ ... ΚΟΛ
ΣΤΟ ΦΩΘΟΝΕ
CΤΟΥ ... ΟΥΗ
ΚΩCΜ ... ΠΑCΕ

Deisis icon,
Bachkovo Monastery (1495).
Old Bulgarian Art section,
Crypt of the St Alexander
Nevsky Cathedral

The Nativity: fresco, Holy Archangels Church,
the village of Arbanassi, 18th C

Rila Monastery. Established in the middle of the 10th C, by the anchorite St Ivan of Rila. One of the leading educa-tional, literary and spiritual centres in Bulgaria

A street in Koprivshtitsa, a well developed cultural and economic centre in the 19th C

A typical rich merchant's house in Plovdiv (18th-19th C.), now turned into an ethnographic museum

The Virgin Hodegetria early 19th C. Toma Vishanov,
Bansko school, 67/46, tempera. The Church of Archangel
Michael in the village of Ossenovo, Bansko region

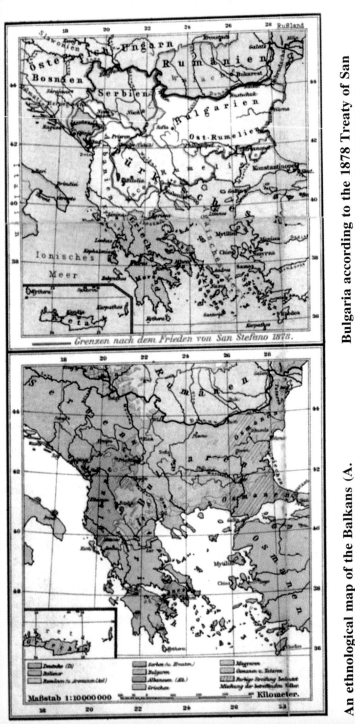

Bulgaria according to the 1878 Treaty of San Stefano and according to the 1878 Berlin Treaty. (A.Velhagen & A.Klasing)

An ethnological map of the Balkans (A. Velhagen & A.Klasing)

**Veliko Turnovo,
where the First Grand National
Assembly sat in 1879**

The centre of Sofia. The National Assembly building (right) and the St Alexander Nevsky Cathedral

insula for the first time, which reinforced the conviction of the Christians that their only hope for liberation lay in the north, in Russia.

The wars with Russia and Austria were a new wake-up call to the Empire. New attempts to carry out reforms were made by Sultan Selim III (1789–1808), who desperately tried to create a modern army, get rid of the unruly Janissary Corps and the complacent spahis, the irregular cavalry. This new attempt failed like the previous one.

The crisis was at its height in the late 18th Century. The central government was unable to control its territories and maintain order. Individual local rulers rebelled in the North African territories, in Egypt and in the Middle East, making Turkish rule purely nominal. In the Balkans, several powerful military leaders established independent principalities over which the central government had no control. The best known example is the Vidin ruler Osman Pazvantoglu, who annexed to his domain half of Northern Bulgaria. His self-confidence was so great that he pursued his own foreign policy and was in correspondence with Napoleon Bonaparte of France. There was a second, more dramatic side to political separatism: chaos. Lack of control over the Ottoman territories and the collapse of the spahi system left a huge army of idle soldiers on the roads, people without jobs and property who made robbery their only means of livelihood. Organised in gangs, those bandits scourged the Balkans. The helplessness of central authority became manifest in its most desperate step: it allowed Christians to carry arms for the first time in three centuries. In this troubled time, Bulgaria entered a new era – the National Revival Era.

The Bulgarian Revival

The European powers tangibly changed their attitude to the weakening Ottoman Empire. As Europe industrialised, its needs for raw materials and food grew and it set its sights on the southeastern corner of the continent. Thus the Balkans entered the sphere of European interests as a source of raw materials controlled by an empire whose sovereignty was on the decline, and hence an attractive target for economic invasion. Each unsuccessful war of the Ottoman Empire was followed by more trade concessions to allies and enemies alike.

The most fascinating phenomenon in Bulgarian history in the 18th and 19th Centuries was not so much political life as the momentous change in mentality and behaviour, i.e. modernisation. The humble Balkan man, whose ancestors had grazed their sheep or dyed wool, left his family and the comparatively calm undemanding life in some quiet valley to travel hundreds of kilometres to sell his sheep or wool. Now there were people imbued with the spirit of enterprise, who were ready to brave the dangerous roads, highwaymen and the corrupt authorities, in quest of a better life. While the Ottoman Empire was a clenched fist banging on the doors of Europe, the subjects' opportunities for private enterprise were minimal. But now that the grip was loosening, the Bulgarians were quick to act and took the dangerous but rewarding road of entrepreneurship.

Slow but far-reaching changes began in agriculture, the most important sector of the economy at the time. Large market-oriented farms (*chifliks*) emerged. New crops were introduced for the first time in several centuries: maize, which was seen as yet another whim of the Turks at first, only to be appreciated as food and animal feed later on; and cotton, which was needed in huge quantities for the boom in the European textile industry. Tobacco was grown in large fields in the southern Bulgarian lands – Southeastern Thrace, the valley of the Strouma River and the Rhodope Mountains, where it has been the most important crop ever since. Trade picked up, becoming an accessible source of quick profit. Local markets evolved into seasonal fairs – the first commodity exchanges, which drew merchants from far-off places.

The huge market of the Empire – from the Adriatic coast to Mesopotamia and Egypt was a major advantage for Bulgarian merchants. The capital, Istanbul, with a population of nearly one million was a huge centre of consumption for the Balkan provinces' merchandise. Bulgarian merchants and goods took the long-charted roads to Russia, Wallachia and Moldova, Vienna and Budapest. Local industry, however, developed at a much slower pace because of the absolute domination of artisan production. At the end of the 18th Century the guilds were thriving under the patronage of the central government. Nevertheless, rigorous thrift and 14-hour working days helped Bulgarian artisans achieve modest prosperity.

After the turmoil at the beginning of the century, the economic and social climate began to improve in the 1820s–30s and the Empire entered a period of relative stability. The reforms launched by Sultan Mahmud II (1808–1839) and his successors were a serious attempt to follow the European model. In 1826 the Sultan planned and pushed through the boldest reform, disbanding and killing the parasitic and disobedient Janissary Corps. Unprecedented economic growth in Europe in the 1860s–70s had a positive effect on the Ottoman provinces. The Crimean War of 1853–1856, in which Turkey together with France and Britain, inflicted a crushing defeat on Russia,was a new political disappointment to the Bulgarians, but it also brought a handsome profit from military supplies. Artisanal production made considerable progress amid the general upsurge in the economy. The use of water energy became increasingly widespread, being the only accessible energy source in the technologically backward Empire. The first real industrial enterprises appeared in this favourable environment. The first textile mill opened in 1834 but did not operate properly until after the war. The first railways were built entirely with foreign (British and Austrian) capital, and by the mid-1870s there were over 2,000 kilometres of railways, of which 1,000 kilometres were on Bulgarian land.

One of the most difficult problems was to modernise the financial system of the Empire, Bulgaria included. The internal and trade deficits were enormous. There was galloping inflation – in thirty-one years Sultan Mahmud II allowed a 72-fold devaluation of the coins, which further aggravated the unstable financial situation. Another problem was the complicated currency system: the Empire used both local currency units (the piastre and the gros) and European ones (Austrian thalers and Russian rubles). An attempt was made in 1863 to solve the financial problems by establishing the Ottoman Imperial Bank, the first modern financial institution, with French and British capital. It gradually turned into a bank of issue. The 1860s saw the formation of the first joint-stock credit companies with Bulgarian participation, whose number reached forty. But the financial crisis grew out of control and in the 1870s the Empire declared bankruptcy.

The economic upheaval inevitably caused changes in Bulgarian society. The stabilisation of the state and more comfortable life led to an increase in the birth rate. Experts say that before the Liberation in 1878, the Bulgarian population of the Ottoman Empire numbered 5 to 5.5 million people.

A new social structure took shape between the 1820s and the 1970s. The majority of the population, nearly 80 per cent, were peasants who owned or used land. They formed the backbone of Bulgarian society. The proportion of Bulgarian artisans, who were the most dynamic social group, rose, and so did their social status. Along with merchants, they were the driving force behind the changes which shaped the Bulgarian Revival.

Within the Ottoman Empire, the Bulgarian economic elite consisted of merchants and usurers. There was a larger or smaller number of well-off or even rich families in each Bulgarian town. Trade was their basic occupation, but they were ready to take up anything that promised to bring in a handsome profit. New social groups emerged in Bulgarian society in the 19th Century. The number of Bulgarian clerks employed in the administration and the government was on the rise. The fledgling intelligentsia, a new, comparatively small group, played a major role in national life. Initially consisting of teachers and clergy, it was joined by the first Bulgarian medical doctors, journalists and editors as education developed and training abroad became more accessible. The increased activity of the population gradually changed the organisation of Bulgarian municipalities. Village mayors, guild councils and parish councillors began to carry more weight with both local people and the Ottoman authorities, and were, in effect, implementing local government. An important sign of modernisation was the growth of towns. They became increasingly attractive with the opportunities they offered, drawing a wave of poor mountain villagers seeking a better life. By 1878, town dwellers made up one-fifth of the Bulgarian population. By the mid-19th Century there were at least half a dozen towns with a population of 15,000 to 30,000 each. New elegant houses built the town centres combining Oriental luxury with European elegance. Smart horse-drawn carriages and clothes styled in Vienna were shown off in the streets by the well-to-do. East and West met in the Bulgarian towns. Sitting near mosques and in coffee shops, old Turks puffed quietly at their pipes, steeped in Oriental languor, while several blocks away a dance was being held at a Christian home.

A new reality was emerging in the 18th and 19th Centuries. The Bulgarian lands, which had echoed with the thump of marching armies for three centuries, were coming alive as the pulsating arteries of trade sent fresh blood to each settlement. It was a slow but irreversible awakening. A change in mentality and behaviour followed in the wake of economic and social progress.

The making of a nation

The process of consolidation of the Bulgarian ethnic and regional groups in a single national community paralleled social evolution in the rest of Europe. Culture played a dramatic role, providing the framework within which the new elements of individual and group identity were conceived, rationalised and established. While Bulgarian society was on its way to cultural maturity, literature was the arena of the first national insights and the first battles for establishing a national identity since it was the spiritual product which had kept the link with the medieval tradition alive for centuries.

Spiritual revival was indisputably a nationwide phenomenon. As elsewhere in the world, this process is represented and symbolised by several outstanding figures,who gave a face and a name to the early cultural revival. The most prominent figure is Paissii of Chiliandari (Paissiy Hilendarski). Born around 1722 in Bansko, a small town in Southwestern Bulgaria, he became a monk in a Mount Athos monastery. There he found himself amidst a rekindled rivalry between Bulgarians and Greeks, with the latter exploiting the Bulgarians' lack of recorded history. In 1762 Paissii wrote his Slav-Bulgarian History which became the manifesto of the Bulgarian National Revival. Paissii wrote that small book inspired by a desire to tell the whole story of the Bulgarian past and restore for the people the lost link with its history. He revived the memory of the medieval Bulgarian state, thus providing the necessary starting point for the Bulgarian cultural revival. The thin manuscript had an impressive effect. Obviously, the History appeared at the right time and reached the right people. It was seen as a revelation. The first hand-written copy was made in 1765 and several dozen copies have survived.

The cultural changes in Bulgarian society signalled by Paissii's history and the keen interest it aroused extended beyond the awakened interest in historical reading. One field where the changes were particularly marked was education. Religious schools where children studied the Scriptures had met the modest need for literacy for centuries, but in the late 18th Century their deficiencies became obvious. There were attempts to transform the traditional monastery cell schools: the number of schoolchildren increased and even girls were admitted; the basics of arithmetic and geography were introduced. A major step forward was the opening of municipal schools financed by the whole parish, which marked the transition of education from the private to the public sphere. The most important innovation was the secular school where primers replaced prayer-books and teaching was done in the vernacular. The first modern Bulgarian school opened in the town of Gabrovo in the Balkan Mountains in 1835 with a donation provided by wealthy Bulgarian immigrants. The first all-girls school opened in Pleven, in Northern Bulgaria, in 1840.

The importance of the opening of secular schools in Bulgaria defies overestimation. New-style education changed the foundations of culture: the outlook on the world and man, and the connection between them. These concepts had been part of a comprehensive cultural model, partly Christian and partly mythological, for centuries in

Bulgarian society. But there was more to the transition from traditional to modern society than economic and social change; the popular mentality also took a quantum leap. Suddenly, the world was round, vast and diverse, and schools armed their pupils with knowledge and understanding of it. Modern schools taught a new generation which had access to the latest European achievements in knowledge about the world. The first Bulgarian graduates of European universities returned home to become teachers. By 1878 Bulgaria had over 2,000 schools. What Bulgarians created was not just schools, but a unique national education system which, despite all difficulties and obstacles, illusions and failures, drove society forward. The new Bulgarian school was the driving force behind two vital processes: the modernisation of society and the consolidation of the Bulgarian nation.

Economic, social and cultural development reached its height in the third quarter of the 19th Century, which can be termed the Mature Revival. The closed society of the 16th and 17th Centuries had turned into a seething national community which eagerly adopted 19th-century achievements. The formation of civic organisations – reading clubs and societies – was an important development which facilitated access to the fruits of civilisation. 1856 saw the birth of the Bulgarian theatre and its enthusiastic audience. The first women's societies were set up, which was no mean achievement in an Islamic empire and a society where women were not allowed to show their hair, let alone their interests. As printing developed, the first Bulgarian book-shops opened in Plovdiv and Rousse, which were also clubs of young intellectuals. A Bulgarian Literary Society was set up in 1869, which developed into the Bulgarian Academy of Sciences after the Liberation.

One of the most important signals that the perception of the world had changed was the creation of fiction and art, and the manifestation of a new aesthetic attitude to the world. The Holy Scriptures and icons were part of the religious experience. The modern age brought cultural consumption and individualism. Sofronii, Bishop of Vratsa (1739–1813), wrote the autobiographic "Life and Ordeal", whose protagonist is an ordinary man, not a saint. The basic forms and genres of modern Bulgarian literature emerged one after another. Poetry became a favourite genre of the Bulgarian intellectuals and nearly all literate people dabbled with rhymes. In other fields it took a longer time for elements of modern culture to replace the traditional ones. Although European music was played at some homes, folk songs and dances were strongly preferred by villagers and townspeople alike. Most artists were nothing more than icon painters, who followed century-old models. But in the fine arts, too, there were marked changes. Several centres of religious painting took shape in the 18th Century in the small mountain towns of Samokov, Bansko and Tryavna. Their numerous representatives breathed life into the ultra-conservative Orthodox tradition: the portrayed figures were infused with human intensity, the colours were brighter and of a wider spectrum. The most interesting figure among Bulgarian icon painters, Zahari Zograph of Samokov, worked in many places in the 1840s and 50s. The faces in his frescoes are touched with individuality and the still images with emotion; what is more, the features of real people are incorporated in them (e.g. the series of portraits of rich Plovdiv residents painted in the Bachkovo Monastery). Zahari Zograph offered a new interpretation of traditional subjects ("The Wheel of Life" in the Transfiguration Monastery near Turnovo) and even painted a self-portrait, which signalled the emergence of the self-confidence of the artist who was no longer an artisan. One of the first professional modern artists, Stanislav Dospevski, was a relative of Zograph. He and Nikolay Pavlovich were the first Bulgarians to receive formal artistic training abroad. Curiously, their portraits scared prospective buyers with their realism for a long time. Modern art forms, initially meeting mistrust and criticised as being immoral and atheistic, gradually laid the groundwork for the post-Liberation modern Bulgarian culture.

While it followed modern European models, 19th-century Bulgarian culture had many distinctive features. One of them was its profoundly secular character and quick departure from religion to ostensible atheism. Given the lack of a strong theological tradition and the specifically practical nature of Christianity in the Bulgarian lands, there was no environment for a serious religious culture similar to that of Western Europe. Another characteristic feature of Bulgarian culture during the National Revival was its relative homogeneity. No elitist culture evolved because there was no national elite with established traditions among the Bulgarians. Nearly all strata of society used the same national cultural sources and no cultural chasms opened between the classes and social strata. Literature, the fine arts and education were primarily instruments of national consolidation and fast Europeanisation.

From national ideas to national action

The growing prosperity and tangible cultural progress of the Bulgarian Christian communities accelerated national consolidation. The enthusiasm grounded in the newly discovered national consciousness gradually turned into a need for national recognition. In the spirit of nationalism which dominated Europe throughout the 19th Century, the Bulgarians took action to become culturally and politically independent. Insofar as self-identification presupposes, first and foremost, differentiation from others, the Bulgarian national movement originated in religion. Like the Reformation in Europe in the early 16th Century, the Bulgarian church movement was essentially a struggle for a people's church.

From the 15th Century onwards, the senior Christian clergy in the Ottoman Empire had consisted of Greeks, who, along with their utter corruption, were taken for granted until the emergence of the Greek national doctrine. In the mid-18th Century the conservative ultra-Greek policy of the Patriarchate of Constantinople was confronted by the Bulgarians' growing national self-confidence and their aspirations to be recognised as a nation on an equal footing with the other nations. The long smouldering animosity burst into open conflicts. The1820s saw open clashes over the election of senior clerics and the language of religious services: Bulgarian or Greek.This essentially political and national conflict used legal instruments such as official complaints, objections and petitions. The most farsighted Bulgarians quickly saw the need for joint action in what was then the decision-making centre – Istanbul. In the 1840s it had a sizeable Bulgarian colony. Contemporary researchers estimated that at least 50,000 Bulgarian artisans and merchants lived permanently or temporarily in the capital of the Empire. In 1844 two Bulgarian clerics – Neofit Bozveli and Ilarion Makariopolski – handed the Istanbul authorities a proposal for improving the position of the Bulgarian population. It included demands for elective senior Bulgarian clerics in the Bulgarian eparchies, for the opening of Bulgarian schools, for books and textbooks to be published in Bulgarian, and for a Bulgarian church in Istanbul. In spite of the guarded wording and modest demands, the petition was, in effect, a programme for Bulgarian national and cultural autonomy. This is how the Patriarchate and the Istanbul authorities saw it, too. It was turned down and the two petitioners were exiled to Mount Athos. The church question entered its decisive phase in the 1860s when the people in many places openly and unambiguously confronted the Greek Metropolitans. In 1859 in a Plovdiv church the dispute about the language of religious services led to a scuffle, in which the parishioners prevailed using icons, chairs and candelabra. In the late1860s the Bulgarians in the eparchies effectively broke with the Greek clergy. Despite the protests of the Patriarchate, on February 28, 1870, the Sultan's Chancellery issued a firman on the establishment of an independent Bulgarian church headed by an exarch based in Istanbul and comprising most Bulgarian eparchies. The firman envisaged holding a plebiscite in mixed-population regions in Macedonia, where people clearly stated their affiliation with the Bulgarian Church. The establishment of an independent Bulgarian Church came as a formal recognition of an obvious fact: the Bulgarians inhabiting large areas of the European territories of the Ottoman Empire and who were not quite clearly distinguished from other Christian subjects, had gradually evolved into a modern nation. Bulgarian cultural and historical unity had become a fact. Their separation into an independent political community became the immediate national goal.

In the decades when the majority of Bulgarian town dwellers were trying to open their own schools and the first Bulgarian leaders came across the most obvious obstacle to national recognition, the Greek church hierarchy, a small group of single-minded patriots looked far into the future. To the most radical of them, the achievements in education and success in the fight against the intrigues of the Patriarchate were a poor remedy for the Bulgarian problems. The Bulgarians made several attempts, albeit isolated and premature, to solve once and for all the Bulgarian problem by taking up arms against Ottoman rule as the Serbs and the Greeks had done. Bulgarian detachments took part in the Greek and Serbian revolts in the early 19th Century, as well as in each Russo-Turkish war waged in the Balkans. In 1835 a group of Bulgarians deeply dissatisfied with the latest developments made an attempt at organising a conspiracy in the old Bulgarian capital, Turnovo. There was unrest in Nis and Pirot in1839, followed two years later by an uprising which ended in a massacre and left 200 villages burnt or razed to the ground. Reports on the uprising and its suppression were so terrifying that they prompted an inquiry by an ad hoc European commission. The troubled region was visited by the French economist Jerome Blanqui, who described blood-curdling details of the massacre in a book.

After the end of the Napoleonic wars, the European Great Powers were determined not to allow any more changes on the political map of the continent. After the Edirne peace of 1829 which recognised the separation of Serbia and Greece from the Ottoman Empire, the Great Powers decided that the resulting state of affairs was satisfactory and was to be maintained at any cost. This view on the future of the Empire was most unfavourable for the Bulgarians. Every attempt to raise the Bulgarian question, every revolt drew opposition and was seen as an unnecessary threat to the status quo.

Around the middle of the 19th Century popular discontent with the hostile and corrupt central authority mingled with the Bulgarians' growing national self-confidence, the turmoil surrounding the struggle for an independent church and the growing awareness of the role of power politics.

It was in the wake of these changed circumstances that the first serious attempts to find a political solution to the Bulgarian question were made. The Bulgarians' economic progress and enterprise clashed with the backwardness and opposition of imperial politics. The government squeezed as much revenue as possible from the Bulgarian provinces without providing any defence, patronage of the local economy or conditions for a normal life. All this further alienated the Bulgarians from central authority. Political independence was no longer a Utopian idea, but a possibility exploited by the Serbs and the Greeks. Influenced by European social thinkers and civilisation and no longer fearing for their life and property, Bulgarian emi-

gres showed political resolve to take action. The first attempts to formulate a programme and set up an
organisation for political action were made after the
CrimeanWar (1853–1856) and are associated with the
name of Georgi Rakovski. He drew up the first national
liberation programme in 1858, published political newspapers and even took advantage of the Serbo-Turkish conflicts to form and train a unit of armed rebels. Rakovski
was the first Bulgarian politician to see Balkan cooperation as a means of solving the Balkan states' problems.
His influence and propaganda led to the entry of armed
units into the Bulgarian lands in 1867 and 1868, which
had a limited military effect but a strong psychological
impact.

Vassil Levski, recognised as a national hero by all Bulgarians, mapped out a new national liberation strategy. In
the late 1860s and early 1870s he crossed the Bulgarian
lands setting up committees since he believed that Bulgaria must be liberated through a nationwide uprising.
Bulgarian emigres also stirred themselves to take action.
Their leader, Lyuben Karavelov, drew up a new national
liberation programme which emphasised the Bulgarians'
intention "to live in accord with all their neighbours, not
coveting what belongs to others and standing up for what
is their own". A network of committees was built across
Thrace and Northern Bulgaria by the middle of 1871,
whose activities were co-ordinated by a Bulgarian Central
Revolutionary Committee based in Bucharest. Unfortunately, treachery led to Vassil Levski's arrest and hanging,
which dealt a fatal blow to the core of the revolutionary
organisation, its internal network. It took several years to
end the standstill.

The situation in the Balkans deteriorated again in the
summer of 1875 when Bosnia and Herzegovina, openly
supported by Montenegro, rose against Ottoman rule.The
Eastern Question, which the Great Powers had considered

settled, foiled their plans again. Bulgarian revolutionary immigrants took the conflict as a sign that the people must take resolute action, and tried to incite an uprising in September 1875. A high price was paid for this premature attempt: more than 600 people were arrested and 60 sentenced, seven with the death penalty. Failure did not discourage the emigres, who set up a new committee in November 1875 and fixed a date for a new uprising. Active but uncoordinated preparations began. In regions such as Plovdiv and Turnovo the whole population was involved: some stockpiled arms and cast bullets, others sewed uniforms. Some even made wooden cannons. However, the majority of the population remained outside the organisation.

Unforeseen circumstances – one of the conspirators turned traitor – caused the uprising to break out prematurely in Koprivshtitsa, a small town in the foothills of the Balkan Mountains, on April 20, 1876. In a couple of days it spread across Plovdiv district, except for the bigger towns of Plovdiv and Pazardjik which had strong Turkish garrisons.

The Porte set out to crush the uprising with fearful barbarity. Not only did the government send large regular troops to the rebel areas, but it called on local Muslims to form bands and fight the insurgents. The main centres of resistance fell and the suppression was quick and bloody: the rebel villages were looted and burned down and the people massacred. Fires were burning all along the Upper Maritza valley. Nearly all the leaders died tragically. In a few days, when the outcome was already clear, rebel forces engaged in desperate fighting around Turnovo. Northwestern Bulgaria witnessed the tragic ending. A group of freedom-fighters led by poet revolutionary Hristo Botev entered Bulgaria at Kozloduy on the Danube on May 17 and engaged Turkish forces. This act of self-sacrifice was intended to draw the attention of the outside world to Bulgaria. The consequences of the April Uprising were tragic:

tens of thousands of people were killed, dozens of villages razed to the ground and flourishing towns burned down. The sacrifice was not made in vain, however. Looking at the blazing fires, Georgi Benkovski, one of the leaders of the uprising, uttered the prophetic words: "I have achieved my aim! I have inflicted a bleeding wound in the tyrant's heart which will never heal."

Though crushed, the April Uprising triggered off a chain of events as a result of which the rebels' cherished dream came true: a free Bulgaria. The events of 1876 and the first reports on the victims provoked a storm of indignation, which was probably strongest in Russia. Dispatches from the European consuls and ambassadors brought to Turkey's European territories newspaper correspondents seeking the truth. Articles by American journalist J. A. MacGahan and by Frenchman Jean du Vestine depicted an appalling picture of atrocities, unthinkable in the "humanistic" 19th Century: 30,000 people killed or missing, hundreds of burned settlements. The strong international response and public pressure forced the Great Powers to seek ways to settle the crisis. When diplomatic efforts failed, Russia began preparing for war. Tsar Alexander II issued a manifesto declaring war on Turkey on April 12, 1877. The main Russian forces crossed the Danube at Svishtov on June 15, 1877. Bulgarians all over the country were overjoyed to welcome the Russians, seeing that a long-cherished dream was coming true and Russia, endearingly called "Grandpa Ivan", had come to their assistance. The Russian troops quickly liberated the central part of Northern Bulgaria and crossed the Balkan Mountains, where their advance was checked by a strong army led by Suleiman Pasha. They retired to the Shipka Pass, where 5,500 Russians and Bulgarian volunteers held out against the attacks of a 27,000-strong Turkish army for three days, which tactically decided the Russians' success. The fall of the heavily fortified Pleven and the liberation of Sofia paved the way to

Istanbul. The Porte had to sign a peace treaty in San Stefano, a small town near Istanbul, on March 3, 1878, declaring unconditional surrender.

The provisional peace treaty recognised an independent Bulgaria within its ethnic borders, which exceeded the Bulgarians' wildest dreams. However, this success of Russian politics and the establishment of a strong Slavic state in the centre of the Balkan Peninsula angered the West European Powers and Bulgaria's Balkan neighbours. The Western governments were adamantly opposed to the provisions of the treaty, Turkey refused to implement it, and Britain threatened to go to war with Russia. German Chancellor Bismarck invited the parties to deliberate on the issue in Berlin and reach a settlement. Russia was forced to make concessions. The Congress held from June 13 to July 13 ended with the signing of theTreaty of Berlin which considerably altered the earlier decisions. Instead of a unified Bulgaria, a Principality of Bulgaria was set up to encompass Northern Bulgaria and the Sofia region, and an autonomous province of Eastern Rumelia, subject to the Sultan, south of the Balkans was created. Certain territories west of Sofia were given to Serbia, and Northern Dobroudja to Rumania. Turkey retained Macedonia. The decisions of the Berlin Congress satisfied the Western Powers but left the Balkan states bitterly disappointed. The Bulgarians achieved their aim, an independent state, only to find themselves divided again. The return of entire provinces to Turkey paved the way for new struggles for liberation, and the unresolved territorial issues were a time bomb threatening peace in the Balkans for decades to come.

IX. BULGARIA BETWEEN THE HOPE AND THE DISILLUSIONMENT (1878–1944)

A difficult start

Bulgaria emerged as a modern state on the map of Europe with a burdensome heritage. The Berlin Congress defeated the euphoria of the liberation. Instead of the desired unification of all lands inhabited by Bulgarians (about 170,000 square kilometres), the Principality of Bulgaria, born at the Congress, got only 63,752 sq. km. The whole of the subsequent history of Bulgaria can be understood only through the prism of the "holy" struggle for the unification of all Bulgarians.

Despite the painful trauma, life went on. Back in the years of the Revival, Bulgarian society had made its big choice: to become westernised. Modernisation, understood as Europeanisation, meant conscious pursuit of the model set by Western Europe: private ownership and entrepreneurship, modern infrastructure, democratic procedures in political life and guarantees for the basic human rights and liberties. These formed the ideology of the first Bulgarian Constitution adopted in 1879.

With the document establishing the Principality of Bulgaria signed, next on the agenda came a huge and complex problem: how to build a new and totally different economic and political system on the ruins of the Ottoman Empire. The newly emerged state had neither traditions nor qualified people, and lacked the basic know-how for the making of a modern state. The initial momentum came from the Russian Bureau for Civil Government of Liberated Land that was set up before the war of 1877–1878 and that employed experienced administrators. Unusual for a Russian nobleman and a civil servant, Prince Cherkaski who headed the Bureau, prioritised local self-government from the very start of his work. Bulgarian police, administration and judicial staff were appointed in all newly liberated Bulgarian towns.

The Berlin Treaty stipulated that Russian troops and authorities could stay in the Principality for only nine months. A great deal was achieved in this period of less than a year from August 1878 to February 1879: collection of taxes started to provide the fuel for the state machinery, adequate postal and communications services were established and clerks were recruited. A military school was opened, as well as a national bank and a national library to act as the three pillars of future Bulgaria. Following a debate, Sofia was chosen as the capital city because of its strategic location and in view of the future unification of the Bulgarian lands in Moesia, Thrace and Macedonia.

The birth of modern Bulgaria

On February 10, 1879, Turnovo became the venue of a Constituent Assembly whose task was to adopt the basic principles of the building of the new Bulgarian state – the Constitution. Apart from Bulgarians, sitting in the Constituent Assembly were representatives of the Turkish, Greek and Jewish minorities (229 delegates), a proof of the ethnic and religious tolerance that was to dominate the whole of subsequent Bulgarian history. The draft constitution stirred up the first heated debates: for and against the monarchy, for and against civil liberties. The Conservatives claimed that after the long foreign domination Bulgarians lacked political experience; therefore, without a strong monarch's institution destructive instincts and behaviour might come to prevail. The so called Liberals were not so much against the monarchy but just sought to curtail the future prince's powers and reserve greater weight for Parliament. The Liberals took the upper hand in the debate. The Constitution of Turnovo was signed on April 16, 1879. It established democratic order and became one of the most liberal constitutions Europe had seen by the end of the 19th Century. Thus Bulgaria became a constitutional monarchy where power was concentrated in a unicameral National Assembly (Parliament) which drafted laws, approved the national budget and controlled the executive. The National Assembly was elected through universal male suffrage. Bulgaria further adopted broad limits of self-administration and impressive civil rights and liberties. The Prince of Bulgaria still had limited jurisdiction. He was a symbol of national unity, represented the country in its international relations and was Supreme Commander-in-Chief of the Bulgarian armed forces.

The first Prince of the new Principality of Bulgaria was Alexander of Battenberg, a German officer and nobleman. He took power in a European compromise. The Prince enjoyed the support of Russia, the favours of Britain and France and co-operation from Austria-Hungary and Germany. This had its weak point, however, for he had to be at once loyal to Russia, compliant with Britain and France, well disposed to Austria and Germany and still obedient to his formal suzerain – the Sultan.

Alexander of Battenberg (1857–93). The first Prince of Bulgaria. Born in 1857 in the family of Prince Alexander von Hesse-Darmstadt (the brother of Russian Tsarina Maria Alexandrovna) and his morganatic wife Countess Julia von Haucke. Prince Alexander was nephew and godchild of the Russian Emperor Alexander II (Romanov) and was put on the Bulgarian throne with his warmest approval. Later on the Prince entered into a conflict with his cousin, the Russian Emperor Alexander III and was deposed on his orders.He returned to his country where he married an opera singer and served in the Austrian army. He died in 1893.

Bulgaria on the road to independent political development

Within several months only, the first Bulgarian governments made impressive strides toward laying the groundwork of a modern European state. Between 1880 and 1881, two Liberal governments came one after the other and the country saw the passage of a series of major laws: the Electoral Law (one of the most liberal in Europe), the Administrative Division Act which opened up broad vistas for local self-government and the Encouragement of Agriculture Act aimed at consolidating the economic foundations of the country. All this did not go without problems. The first seven years of the young state were filled with serious political and interpersonal skirmishes.The formation of the state elite was delayed by the continuing Ottoman domination over part of Bulgaria. This awareness of going too slow led to greed for power and fast profit, severe infighting and rampant corruption, jeopardising the future of the Principality. In this dangerous environment the monarch was the only figure who could act as an indispensable and reliable regulator.

Trying to do exactly this, the Prince dissolved Parliament in 1881, revoked the Constitution and following elections for a Grand National Assembly got seven-year extraordinary prerogatives. The aim of this extreme step was to establish a centralised government, and eliminate partisan infighting and thus pave the way for a strong and stable state. The regime of prerogatives remains one of the most controversial chapters in the early history of modern Bulgaria. Under the pressure of public discontent in 1883 Battenberg terminated the regime and restored constitutional government. Despite controversial evaluations of his rule, Prince Alexander of Battenberg doubtlessly did his best to provide the conditions for Bulgaria to embrace the modern standards of European statehood. Important new ministries were set up, including the Ministry of Public Buildings, Agriculture and Commerce (1882) which was to see to and encourage the progress of the Bulgarian economy. A European-style financial and taxation organisation was introduced; the hateful tithe was eliminated; a National Census Bureau and a National Accounting Office were established. The judiciary was stabilised through the Judiciary Constitution Act. The important Government Employees' Provisory Regulations were enacted to provide the groundwork for an independent, professional and competent government apparatus. Even in advanced countries such as Britain this problem had been resolved only in the late 1860s.

The armed forces received special attention in the overall drive for improvement. They grew into the most advanced, best equipped and most expertly commanded army in the Balkans at the end of the 19th Century and especially in the first decade of the 20th Century. It was seen as a major instrument for achieving the aspirations for the unification of the nation.

The situation was more delicate with regard to the international relations of the Principality of Bulgaria. Being the largest ethnic group in terms of population and territory, the Bulgarians were looked upon by their neighbours with fear and resentment. Located on the inland and sea corridor to the Bosphorus and the Dardanelles straits, and the Eastern Mediterranean, the Bulgarian state was central to the interests of the Great Powers. Apart from being a model of cultural grandeur to be imitated, Europe has always been a decisive factor in the success or failure of any foreign policy step taken by Bulgaria.

The first such step was aimed at the unification of the Principality of Bulgaria and the autonomous East Rumelia. It was the first occasion for the Bulgarians to show to the world their capacity to organise and maturity as diplomats. These were displayed in the simultaneous building of a stable internal administration, educational establishments and management systems and authorities in East Rumelia, to serve the goals of the Unification.The activists of the Unification, among whom Zachari Stoyanov stood out, managed to neutralise the European idea of turning East Rumelia into an uncomfortable part-Turkish, part-Greek, part-Bulgarian province. Having felt their strength and the tacit support of the Bulgarian government and public, including Prince Battenberg, the leaders of the Unification movement announced the death of East Rumelia and its accession to the Principality of Bulgaria on September 6, 1885 in Plovdiv. Fearing subsequent complications from the violation of the Treaty of Berlin, the Russian Tsar refused to support the Unification thus severely injuring Russia's image in Bulgaria. Despite Russia's refusal to back the undertaking, the Unification was defended with military force against Serbia and arranged through diplomatic channels in early 1886.

The conflict between the monarch on the one side, and the democratic constitution and the public sentiments, on the other, was temporarily quietened by the events surrounding the Unification and the subsequent Bulgarian-Serbian War. Amid national enthusiasm and national euphoria, the Prince was pushed forward by his supporters as the unifier of Bulgaria. Only a year later, on August 9, 1886, a group of officers dissatisfied with the policy of the court, staged a coup d'etat, ousted the prince and declared a regency. The coup was neutralised by other opposition parties which succeeded in taking the upper hand in the fight for power but nonetheless it proved fatal for the young prince who was humiliated and driven away from the country as an inept ruler for whom the crown was too heavy a burden and a person who did not enjoy the favour of the Russian Tsar.

Again, Bulgarians had to tour Europe in search of a new prince. In 1887 they finally selected Ferdinand Saxe-

Coburg-Gotha, a German prince who was related by blood
to many ruling dynasties and yet disliked by the Great Powers. Ferdinand assumed an important post in Bulgarian history with his adventurous policy that brought the country
to a political and economic catastrophe, with his numerous love affairs, extreme arrogance and a big nose which
made him a favourite target for the fledgling Bulgarian art
of political caricature.

**Ferdinand I (1861–1948) (Ferdinand Maximillian Karl
Leopold Maria)** Son of Prince August von Saxe-Coburg-Gotha
and Princess Clementine Orleans, the daughter of French King
Louis-Philippe. He was put on the Bulgarian throne in 1887 caus-
ing a diplomatic scandal. Later he was recognised by the Great
Powers and much later (1896) by Russia. In 1908 he declared
Bulgaria's full independence from the Ottoman Empire and pro-
claimed himself The King of Bulgarians. He is largely consid-
ered to be the culprit for the national catastrophes following the
country's involvement in World War I on the side of the Central
Powers. In 1918 he abdicated to be replaced by his first born son
Boris.

The early years of Ferdinand's rule, however, were
dominated by another figure – Stefan Stambolov, a Liberal and Prime Minister from 1887 to 1892. His iron hand,
clear political vision and concern for the well-being of the
state set Bulgaria onto an ascending line of development
which lasted till the destructive wars of the second half of
the 20th Century. An autocratic ruler, Stambolov enforced
measures aimed at promoting the national economy and
establishing an independent foreign policy. During his term
of office the unbelievable happened: his refusal to obey
Russia severed bilateral diplomatic ties. He had also come
under fire for his manner of dealing with his political foes.
One thing though is beyond dispute – his rule brought the
country the closest it had ever been to the desired Euro-

pean model. After 1894 more moderate political parties took turn in ruling the country reinstating democratic principles but soon they too bowed down to Ferdinand's autocratic regime. In the meantime, Stambolov was assassinated by his political enemies in central Sofia in broad daylight.

By the end of the first decade of the 20th Century Bulgarian political life was dominated by parties descended from the Liberals. Bulgarian liberalism was an interesting phenomenon. Not only was liberal philosophy little known to the fledgling Bulgarian politicians but in some cases it was not even shared by them at all. Bulgarians were a society that had just cast off Turkish despotism and lacked any serious political experience. In the vague idea the Bulgarian villager had about politics the best government was the one that levied no taxes but gave out hearty benefits. And as such a platform was not part of the plans of even the most die-hard radicals, Bulgarian liberalism embarked on a difficult road. The most influential centrist parties invariably assumed popular tags such as "Liberal", "Democratic", "Progressive" and "Popular" and their political behaviour depended on their foreign policy orientation and closeness to the court. The lower middle class along with a large class of producers (rural and urban) provided a breeding ground for the many leftist and radical formations: Agrarian, Social Democratic, Socialist and Communist, to mention but a few. A major issue was the impact of the national question on politics – it had been a Damoclean sword for all governments. *While there were sensible people who recognised political realities, nationalism was so dominant in the public mind that not a single politician hoping for a political future, dared take a pragmatic position.*

Between 1894 and 1912 Bulgaria had a varied political life. The Popular Party (1894–1899) restored good relations with Russia and settled the foreign policy problems while furthering the economic policy of the Liberals. A comeback to power by the Liberals coincided with the world economic crisis of the late 19th Century which in Bulgaria was characterised by unwise measures leading to the first social conflicts: the peasant revolts in some parts of the country. The new environment gave birth to a new political force, the Agrarian Union, which grew into an important factor in Bulgarian political development. It was the first purely peasant political organisation in Europe in the early 20th Century. The Bulgarian Social Democratic Party was set up in 1891.

The first decade of the 20th Century saw the establishment of the personal regime of Prince Ferdinand. He left bourgeois parliamentarianism intact and tried not to encroach on the Constitution but got the most important government agencies under his personal control. In doing this, he was facilitated by the coterie of political parties and the ruthless struggle for power that often involved trampling on constitutional principles and election rigging, eating away public confidence. Rightly assessing the situation, the Prince interfered only with diplomacy, the army and the appointment of government. Throughout his personal regime, the press was extremely free and active with a variety of newspapers that never feared to attack and ridicule even the personality of the ruler. But behind this ostensible democracy the iron fist of the monarch was always felt. None of the parliaments after 1894 served their full life and all governments followed the dictates of Ferdinand, to one extent or another.

The pawn in the big game

The small European states of the late 19th and early 20th Centuries were aware of the fact that their role was that of the pawns on the chessboard of European power politics and Bulgaria was no exception. The national interests at the time were dominated by the idea for the unification of Bulgarians outside the then borders of the motherland, which amounted to annexing of territories inhabited by Bulgarians. Bulgarian foreign policy saw its only chance in the insurmountable conflicts between the Great Powers and the possibility of finding a balance. For this reason, the policy adopted by Stefan Stambolov – ceasing full dependence on Russia and seeking new horizons in closer contact with the more modern industrialised states such as Britain, Germany, France and Austria-Hungary – proved right. Having come under the pressure of conflicting interests, Bulgarian diplomacy had to make difficult manoeuvres which together with the flinching temper of Ferdinand often resulted in dangerous political swings. Bulgaria never staked everything on one political force and ended up alone.

The Bulgarian miracle

In economic terms, Bulgaria remained a state of small and medium-scale farming, the extracting and processing industry dominant and a relatively poorly developed infrastructure. By 1944, 80 per cent of the population lived in villages. Bulgarian society was described as "predominantly peasant" and most of the producers were peasants. Urban dwellers were mostly craftsmen, traders, people employed in the service sector and communications, while industrial workers were a minority. Towns had a clearly identified strata of entrepreneurs, civil servants, intellectuals, freelancers, officers of the reserve, clerics and bigger owners. These were all people who were actively involved in the modernisation of the country. They formed the backbone of the political parties and were the founders and major participants in public organisations and cultural institutions.

The diligent reader will remember that pre-liberation Bulgaria had a similar structure. This absolute domination of the rural economy predetermines an unstable political system because the "town parties" that were mushrooming at the time invariably roused suspicions among the village population, while the peasant parties (the Agrarian Union) were unable to rule a modern state. The domination of the village population in Bulgaria also goes to explain why so many of the archaic traditions, ideas, stereotypes and tastes remained in existence for a long time although they had lost much of the original meaning, and put up stiff resistance to the influence of the external new forces. Starting with a technological conservatism and archaic farming practices, the Bulgarian village was only superficially affected by the 20th Century. Even after the forced modernisation under Communist rule, some farms still keep articles of the Neolithic Age such as wooden ploughs, stone grinders, the garbage heap in the back yard and the wood stove. But it was exactly this conservative environment that made it possible to preserve well into the modern culture the traditions, rituals, architecture and applied arts that make up the golden stock of Bulgarian culture.

At the turn of the century the urban economy made a resolute leap forward which brought along new social conflicts and partnerships, new ideologies, political strategies, culture and lifestyles. Industry was gradually stabilised, largely due to the persistent efforts of the governments. 1883 saw the passage of a law placing civil servants under an obligation to wear clothes made of locally produced materials; the Encouragement of Industry Law was passed in 1894 and amended in 1897. 1902 was the onset of a period of prosperity. Till the start of World War I, the number of enterprises rose several-fold, banks multiplied topping the 20-mark by the year 1900, and the first insurance companies emerged. Rail transport was expanding and in

1900 it operated 1,600 km of railways. There were also 6,300 km of roads. Domestic and foreign trade picked up. An exhibition was organised for the first time in Plovdiv in 1892 to evolve into the International Plovdiv Fair that is still held nowadays. From the time of Stambolov to the first decade of the 20th Century Bulgaria lived through its heyday. Surprisingly, its economy overtook those of all other Balkan countries.

Modern cultural institutions started taking shape. A university was founded in 1888, as well as a system of secondary and pedagogical schools, a school of painting, a drama and opera theatre, art galleries, cinemas, scientific, cultural and charitable societies. Bulgarian society was breeding new intellectuals and artists who knew well European culture and held it in high esteem. Among these were the writers and poets Pencho Slaveikov, Aleko Konstantinov, Ivan Vazov and Peyo Yavorov, and the artists Nikola Petrov, Ivan Angelov and Sirak Skitnik. A consistent policy of inviting the best architects led to the emergence of a modern capital city with beautiful private and public buildings, the royal palace, parks and gardens. Only seventeen years after the launching of the world's first electricity-generating plant, Sofia started operating its own hydro-electric power plant at Kokalyane.The Vienna trams were only six years old when the first trams started rattling along the Sofia streets. Bulgaria's first cinema welcomed its first viewers in Rousse (a town on the Danube) five years after the world premiere of the cinematograph.

The period commencing in the early 1890s and ending with Bulgaria's entry into World War I outlined a new reality. Those years came to be known as "The Period of Normality" marked by a stable economy and positive demographic trends, consolidation of the existing social groups and interests, an increasing number of towns acting as the driving force of progress, spreading literacy nation-wide, the formation of an influential intelligentsia and

so on. It was a real *belle époque* for Bulgaria when the
national income was rising, the gold reserve of the national
treasury made the Bulgarian currency convertible and Bulgarians were free to travel and live in Europe as full-
fledged citizens.

The national catastrophes and the end of the good times

The end of The Period of Normality came with the explo-
sion of the time-bomb planted by the Berlin Congress: the
national, territorial and ethnic conflicts in the Balkans.The
Eastern Question, insurmountable and therefore tragic,
became a Damoclean sword for the Balkan nations and
even today continues to impede the normal development
of this much-suffering region. From its very signature, the
Treaty of Berlin caused mass indignation and protests. The
Macedonian population was shocked by its bad luck. Not
only did it remain part of the Ottoman Empire but it also
suffered from the scorn of the Muslims and a large number
of refugees. Threatened by a Bulgaria seeking unification
and an Austria-Hungary rocked by national conflicts,
Serbia hoped to become a Balkan Piedmont. Greece and
Romania added more complexity to the picture of passions
and claims for national grandeur over which the shadow
of the shrinking Ottoman Empire still hung. As Otto von
Bismarck, a seasoned diplomat, put it, if a big war was
ever to start in Europe the spark would come from some
Balkan absurdity. He could not be more right.

The first crisis was prompted by the Unification of Bulgaria. A dramatic reaction came from Serbia which could
not put up with the thought of a greatly enlarged Bulgaria
just across the border. On November 2, 1885, it declared a
war on Bulgaria. Obsessed by the idea of a just cause, the
Bulgarian troops pushed back the Serbian army and en-

tered Serbian territory within a week. Austria-Hungary had to issue a severe threat to stop the Bulgarian offensive. Bulgaria won its first military and diplomatic victory which impressed deeply on some minds the notion that this was the road to achieving the national ideal.

The settling of the Unification showed the Macedonian population that it had been excluded from the plans of the international policy-makers. A quickly spreading unrest entered its decisive phase in the 1890s when a revolutionary organisation was established with the ambition of liberating Macedonia. Two strategies emerged, both yielding unfavourable political results. A faction of the leading figures openly declared that the aim of liberation was accession to Bulgaria. Others more cautiously suggested that the autonomy and development of Macedonia as an independent state was a better option. The organisation grew formulating in detail a programme and documentation, and the tools it would use. One such instrument were detachments of insurgents who campaigned among the people to raise their morale and prepare them for the coming battles. Despite the unfavourable environment, the leaders of the movement took a course towards an insurrection that was to be organised jointly with the separatists of Eastern Thrace. In August 1903, revolts broke out in Macedonia and Eastern Thrace on St. Elijah's Day and Transfiguration Day but soon they were suppressed amid bloodshed.

A second crisis was triggered by the events in Turkey where in 1908 the Young Turks staged a coup d'etat. In the chaos that followed the Macedonian organisations and leaders tried to draw political dividends the only result of which was the murder of more Macedonian leaders and more fratricide.

The crisis of 1908 had two other important aspects in terms of the balance in the Balkans. The Bulgarian Prince and the government decided to capitalise on the unrest and declared the independence of Bulgaria fromTurkey, changing its status from principality to kingdom and making the Bulgarian Prince a King. Austria-Hungary also took advantage of the situation to annex Bosnia and Herzegovina.

These political moves coincided with the formation of the allied blocs in Europe and the open preparation for a major military conflict. In this volatile situation, when war seemed an easy solution to all problems, Bulgaria embarked on a dangerous adventure. Cherishing the memory of the successful Unification, Bulgarian society committed itself to the liberation of its brethren in Macedonia. A powerful patriotic wave mounted, poets started writing militant poems and newspapers campaigned for national unification. Ferdinand saw himself at the helm of a powerful Balkan state, the unifier figure and the successor to the crown of the Byzantine emperors. Bulgaria's neighbours,too, had grand plans and appetites were most naturally connected with the Turkish heritage. Secret treaties for joint military action against Turkey were signed in early1912 with Serbia and Greece. The outbreak of the war was a matter of time. An occasion was found and the First Balkan War broke out on September 17th of the same year. It was a victorious blitz war waged with enthusiasm. A key factor was the high morale of the Bulgarian army which fought with the vision of liberating its "enslaved brethren" and won overwhelming victories over Turkey in the region of Eastern Thrace, capturing the hitherto invincible Edirne fortress. The Treaty of London of May17th, 1913, enshrined the political motto of politicians and the public in Southeastern Europe, "The Balkans – for the Balkan People". And yet the war solved only partially the problem of the national unification of Bulgaria. The controversy about the Macedonian territories which were claimed by Bulgaria, Serbia and Greece at the same time, along with other problems, led to a shift of forces: Serbia allied with Greece and Romania against Bulgaria. Belgrade insisted on respecting the principle of actual occupation which amounted to annexation by Serbia of all lands where the Serbian army had set foot regardless of ethnic or other considerations. The term "Balkanisation" again started to display its sinister connotations. Dazzled by the victories, Ferdinand and his government decided to punish their disloyal allies and made a reckless move attacking first. The Second Balkan War, also known as the War of Allies, was a disaster for Bulgaria. This mistaken move landed the country in its first national catastrophe. Alone against all others, including Romania and Turkey, Bulgaria was defeated and had to pay a high price under the 1913 Treaty of Bucharest. Romania got Southern Dobroudja; Turkey got back Edirne; Serbia acquired the part of Macedonia that had been the Bulgarian share; and Greece kept the Aegean littoral with its best port, Kavalla. Bulgaria was shattered and sunk in complete isolation since all its neighbours – most explicably – feared revenge-seeking. It was the end of the Bulgarian miracle and the beginning of a long era of the pursuit of justice and revenge. Isolated and disgraced, Bulgaria fell easy prey to the Austrian and German diplomacy that found it easy to bond it steadily to the Triple Alliance. A brief peace followed, pregnant with a new war. Everyone had embarked on the road to war and the only question was "when".

An occasion for the European war was found in another Balkan adventure – the assassination of the Austrian heir to the throne by Serbian terrorists. With the war already declared, Bulgaria was subject to pressure both from the Entente (France, Britain and Russia) and the Central Powers (Germany and Austria-Hungary). The Entente offered nothing while Germany offered land and revenge. Ferdinand opted for Germany. Thus Bulgaria once again made the wrong choice and in October 1915 it entered the war on the side of the Central Powers.

In the early stages of the war the Bulgarian army was successful and captured a sizeable part of the desired ter-

ritories in Macedonia and Aegean Thrace. But then the
Entente prevailed. In 1918 after six years of fighting Bulgaria was drained of its powers. The bulk of the male population was mobilised, which reduced drastically the
workforce of the national economy. A subsequent famine
complicated the situation further and hunger riots started
breaking out. There were no supplies for the army and the
soldiers had to wrap their feet with rags to replace the missing boots. A breakthrough by the Entente in Macedonia
forced the Bulgarian troops to withdraw. On the verge of
despair, companies of soldiers dragged along the way to
Sofia. A panicking government first tried to talk them out
of their plans and then sent loyal troops against them. The
battles that followed portended the beginning of a civil war
similar to that in Russia.

Decisive measures had to be taken. A truce was signed,
the government was dissolved and the opposition came to
power. Pointed to as the main culprit for the disaster, Ferdinand abdicated and left the country. He was succeeded
by his son, Boris III. A final peace came with the signing
of the Versailles system of peace treaties while Bulgaria's
status was settled by the Treaty of Neuilly which for the
Bulgarians came to symbolise total defeat. The victorious
states were merciless – the country lost all newly acquired
territories, had to pay huge reparations and contributions
in gold, livestock and foodstuffs, the army was disbanded,
and a stiff and meticulous control was introduced in all
spheres of life. The national catastrophe was complete and
the Bulgarian miracle was done with.

Between the wars: permanent crisis

The wars, the defeats and the Neuilly Peace Treaty changed Bulgarian society for good. A return to normality was
impossible. The government ministers were sentenced, the
Agrarian Union came to power for the first and last time
trying to impose a peasant social Utopia by establishing

social harmony through redistribution of wealth. So-ciety was drained bloodless and morally torn apart. The general pre-war conviction that the road to Europe was the right one, was torpedoed by mistakes in national policy and by the crimes of the winner states whose Neuilly Treaty shaped Bulgaria's history for decades to come.

Without the support of Europe and with burdensome restrictions to obey, Bulgarian society had only two op-tions: autocratic and nationalistic rule or bolshevism. In political life, the period between the two World Wars saw the authoritarian government of the Agrarian Party (1919–1923), its fall in a coup and the establishment of an ex-treme rightist rule after a bloody suppression of the agrar-ians' opposition (1923–1925), temporary liberalisation (1926–1929) interrupted by the Great Depression of 1929, another coup by serving and retired military officers (1934) and the establishment of a pro-totalitarian regime. In the years from 1934 to 1940, the regime established in the coup and the subsequent governments gradually introduced a comprehensive system of laws and ordinances that led to the full centralisation of power and cancellation of demo-cratic freedoms, including a ban on the political parties. In this complex situation the figure of King Boris III stood out as a ruler wielding considerable power. A wise and dexterous politician, obsessed with the idea of stabilisation of the state and overcoming its deep isolation, he was forced to manoeuvre between different political trends while building his personal regime. The political opposi-tion lost its role as a serious corrective to those who ruled the country. The only opposition to the autocratic system came from the leftist forces, inspired, paradoxically, by another totalitarian regime, the Soviet one. The clash be-tween the two ideologies at times bordered on terrorism.

Society was in a crisis also because of the collapse of the national ideals. "National salvation", "National unifi-cation", the national resistance to all enemies, and "Bulgarian, patriotism" were used as mottos by all kinds of political movements and organisations: military, youth, or Macedonian. Art and literature reflected the national crisis as in a mirror. Surprisingly, the movement for a return to the roots of the national art, the cosmopolitan aesthetic platforms and the proletarian art were all deeply rooted in a sense of belonging to nowhere. Pro-Fascist nationalism and proletarian internationalism both attempted to offer an escape from the deep crisis.

Behind the stormy facade of political and intellectual life from the 1930s on, there was a calmer and swifter process of economic development: land allocation and consolidation of the villages, development of a domestic industry, and improvement of the existing infrastructure. By 1939 Bulgaria had reached the pre-war levels, boasting achievements that have remained unrivalled to date. However, it was the 1920s and 1930s that left for future generations some of the best pieces of Bulgarian art, literature and architecture produced by an already mature society. Boris III established himself as "the people's King" who loved driving locomotives and talking to simple people. This gradual stabilisation was harshly interrupted by the new world conflagration.

X. BULGARIA IN THE "SECOND" WORLD

The Second World War and the question of choice

Bulgaria's political fate between the two wars saw it side with Germany – not only ideologically but also in terms of economic, diplomatic and cultural rapprochement. There were many factors which predetermined Bulgaria's position in the new world conflict looming up on the horizon, and left the country with practically no choice. Two of these factors were of particular importance. The first was an objective one: Bulgaria belonged to the group of losers in World War I and had lost territories, economic potential, respect and self-confidence, which were all problems very much familiar to the German nation. Isolated and humiliated, Bulgaria made a natural choice for a partner which was in the same situation and together with which it could seek revision of the Versailles system of peace treaties. With preparation for a war gaining momentum, the enemy camp – that of the European democracies – was eyeing Bulgaria with suspicion and offered no concessions, pushing away from its camp the small Balkan nation. The second factor was that Bulgaria was ruled by a German dynasty which had traditionally good relations with Germany and was related by marriage to the Italian monarchy.

Despite these circumstances, the Bulgarian monarch and most of the Bulgarian public favoured neutrality. Crushed by the burden of the national catastrophes, all wise politicians understood that one could not go against the whole world, albeit under the wing of the Third Reich. Then there emerged a small but influential group of politicians who insisted that Bulgaria should grab its historic chance. For quite a long time Boris III tried to keep Bulgaria out of the conflict. He had to balance between the political and military pressure coming from the Third Reich, the Russophile sentiments of his subjects and the pro-Western orientation of most of the Bulgarian political elite. Brute force took the upper hand. Faced with the aggressive German army marching toward the northern border of the country, Boris III had to form an alliance with Germany. Bulgaria again made its historic choice – unfortunately, the wrong one.

Bulgaria's participation in the war was very limited. The country let in German troops and sent soldiers to Aegean Thrace and Macedonia to seize territories considered essentially Bulgarian. Despite Hitler's pressure, not a single Bulgarian soldier was sent to the Eastern or the Western fronts. Due to strong public opinion and the position of the King, Bulgaria was among the very few countries which did not allow its Jews to be deported to the Nazi death camps.

The years of World War II also saw activity among the leftist forces in Bulgaria. The illegal Communist Party handled its fractional infighting and when Hitler declared war on Russia, it started sabotaging the German army and campaigning for the Soviet cause. In 1943 armed guerrillas went into the mountains and some of them staged successful terrorist acts against German and Bulgarian military bases and vehicles. At that point the government adopted a stiffer approach to the leftist movement, starting mass arrests and introducing the death penalty for Communist conspiracy. Gendarmerie units were formed to chase the Communist guerrillas and in doing so they resorted to public executions and unprecedented atrocities. The victims of this terror became martyrs of the Communist movement and added fuel to the conflict.

Bulgaria's total defeat came before the end of the war. In 1943 the Western allies started bombing Sofia; the country was crashed economically by the regular requisition of food and supplies for the German army. Civil peace was threatened by the fight between the government and the Communists. In early September 1944 the Red Army reached the Danube. The attempts of part of the Bulgarian political elite to get out of the alliance with Germany and avoid a Soviet invasion failed when on September 5th the Soviet Union declared war on Bulgaria and Soviet troops marched into the country. The Communist functionaries staged a coup d'etat and on September 9th the Soviet army triumphantly stood at the helm of Bulgaria.

The long night of Stalinist totalitarianism settled over Bulgaria

The big experiment

The trouble with small nations is that they are rarely the masters of their own fate. At the meeting in Yalta in February 1945 the Big Three (Stalin, Roosevelt and Churchill) drew a line that divided the East and the West and apportioned Russian and Western influence in Bulgaria in the ration of 90:10. In post-war Europe, Bulgaria had the bad luck to fall in Stalin's zone with all the political, economic, social and cultural implications that brought. The political physiognomy of the new regime was epitomised by the so called People's Tribunal instituted in late 1944 and early 1945 to try 135 cases with 11,122 defendants and pass 2,730 death sentences and 8,390 prison sentences of various terms, or property confiscation. The People's Tribunal also tried some representatives of the police and army for atrocities against the guerrillas and that was used as an ideological justification for the trials but the truth is that it was a legal tool for liquidating the nation's political and economic elite.

An Allied Control Commission came to Bulgaria after the war but it had essentially limited functions. The Russian political deputies and the Red Army troops were guarantors of the Communist coup. In the early years the Communist Party ruled on behalf of a broad coalition of parties called the Fatherland Front. All decisions were taken by a democratic mechanism – voting. Elections for a National Assembly were held and they were won (with 88 per cent of the vote) by the Fatherland Front where the Communists had absolute domination. The first government appointed after the elections was not even led by Communists but by loyal representatives of the old political elite. The left modestly took for themselves only the Interior Ministry (i.e. the police) and the Ministry of Justice. A referendum was held in 1946 whereby a striking majority of 95.63 per cent voted to abolish the monarchy and introduce a republican form of government. The regents were brought to court and the royal family, including the infant heir-to-the-throne Simeon, were expelled from Bulgaria. They settled in Spain.

The peace treaty signed in Paris in 1947 was relatively benign as regards the punitive measures against Bulgaria. Big Brother laid a hand over its fledgling ally. After the new realities in Europe were set firmly in place, Bulgaria's new rulers started to implement consistently a programme for restructuring Bulgaria in a Communist spirit. The main tasks were nationalisation of property to the extent of full liquidation of the private sector; radical structural reform of the economy with an emphasis on industry; and mass indoctrination of the ideas of Communism. It was an essentially radical programme for modernisation of the country going beyond the nation's capacity and reasonable limits and involving the abolition of democratic freedoms: a model that was often seen applied in one form or another in the post-war world. The model began to be applied actively in 1947 – the year which marked the beginning of the country's diversion from the normal track of development followed by the other democratic European states.

In 1947 the democratic mask was taken off. A campaign was launched against the opposition with a series of law suits against its leaders. The allies of the Fatherland Front were forced to disband and join one of the few parties allowed to exist: the Workers' (Communists), the Social Democratic (it survived for only several more years) and the left-of-centre pro-Communist faction of the Agrarian Union. A new Constitution was adopted at the end of 1947 and the government was tailored to a Communist model. 1947 also saw the start of nationalisation that swept away first the major industrial enterprises and then large urban properties.

1948 was a new beginning. The first legal Congress of the Communist Party celebrated the end of mimicry and the triumph of a Communist programme, ideology and aims. The party was officially named Communist and from the rostrum of the congress, Georgi Dimitrov, the old party leader who a decade before had become known to the world with the trial where he was accused of setting the Reichstag ablaze, made a speech pronouncing the memorable words that "friendship with the Soviet Union is as necessary for Bulgarians as air and sun for all living beings". In 1948 the Communist movement consolidated and restructured its ranks – in Bulgaria and across the world. The rift between Stalin and Tito and the adoption of a more rigid approach by the so called Communist International Information Bureau marked the beginning of a new era of confrontation. The Berlin events and the erection of the Berlin Wall in 1949 ushered in the era of the Iron Curtain. The Warsaw Pact was established in 1955 to operate as the military organisation of the socialist bloc. For Bulgarian Communist functionaries it was a good time to do away with internal opposition and they started a widely publicised trial against the party traitors. Stalinism triumphed. The last but not least important detail in the picture was the emergence of the "Bulgarian Stalin", Vulko Chervenkov, who started diligently applying the Soviet expertise in worshipping party leaders and denigrating the masses. In political life, the influence of the one-party Stalinist model was disastrous. The chief aim of the new government was to do away with democratic freedoms and the opposition using physical extermination, concentration camps or forcible emigration. The period till the mid 1950s – the last years of Stalin's rule – were dominated by brutal measures to suppress any sign of deviation from the estab-lished dogmas, expropriation of private property and im-planting fear through the establishment of a repressive ap-paratus and a system controlling people's thoughts and behaviour.

1948 saw the launch of an offensive on the economic front. The Party Congress identified the collectivising of land and active industrialisation as topmost priorities. It should be noted that the Communists brought their programme to a successful completion. By the end of the 1950s all land was pooled in co-operative farms and the previous large farms became state-owned. The back-bone of Bulgarian society – small and middle farmers – was crushed. Over a period of 20 years the social structure of the country changed completely. By 1970, 78 per cent of the population had been employed in the non-rural sec-tor and 22 per cent in the rural; 98 per cent of farm land had been included in co-operative or state-owned farms; 80 per cent of Bulgarians lived in urban areas. We should acknowledge, though, that the peasants came to appreciate their new status of complacent mediocrity. Many still talk with nostalgia about the co-operative farms where their efforts were rewarded with payment in kind and hard work and risks were minimised.

Bulgaria built a powerful (much more so than it nee-ded) heavy industry – metallurgy, machine engineering and power generation – which developed in parallel with ore extraction and light industry. In the 1950s, a campaign for developing a domestic industry to reduce external dependence was imprinted deeply in people's minds. Metallurgical giants mushroomed working only with imported ore and coal, and so did machine-building mastodons unable to keep apace with the development of technology. They all survived only due to forcible exports to the other Soviet bloc countries. The Council for Mutual Economic Assistance, or COMECON, that was set up in1949 and was dominated by the Soviet Union, directed the economies of all states symbolised by the economic paradox called "the transferable rouble". In compliance with the COMECON directives of the 1980s, Bulgaria started specialising in the development of high technologies. Tourism became a prosperous business.

Throughout the period of socialist construction, people were subject to huge pressure. Migration, parting with the traditional way of living, low living standards and maddening propaganda nipped people's energy and initiative in the bud. To understand how it is possible to tolerate such an Orwellian society for 50 years, one should be aware of the complex internal dynamics of socialism. After the late 1940s with the post-war poverty and rationing schemes, political persecution, fear and isolation from the rest of the world, there came a period of evolution and things started to improve gradually. In 1956 Stalin's Communism was replaced by the far more demagogic Communism of Todor Zhivkov. Open political persecution was abandoned to be replaced by a system of informers and invisible mechanisms for manipulation. After the shock of collectivisation, farm co-operatives reached pre-war standards of output and living. The chaos and housing crisis in the newly populated cities were overcome through large-scale construction of state-owned housing estates. Further steps were made in the 1960s with the country's opening to the outside world. Some people were sent to business trips in the free world and impressive welfare benefits were granted, including long paid maternity leave, a nation-wide network of day-care centres, cheap vacations, free and relatively good medical services, high and secure pensions, and subsidised prices of almost everything. Special decisions were taken in the early 1970s to boost living standards and improve propaganda, especially among the young. A new generation was growing that remembered nothing about the bourgeois democracy and the war. A new ruling class was taking shape consisting of ruthless and seasoned opportunists who worked with the sole aim of getting rich while reciting perfectly the basics of Communist ideology. Gradually and quietly, they started tolerating the shadow economy, foreign currency trade and Western propaganda. The population was almost 100 percent literate with free access to university education. The intelligentsia was the pet of the Communist regime and enjoyed high prestige, special privileges and a certain freedom of speech as long as what was said stayed inside the writers' cafes. Security instead of freedom, carefully measured doses of consumerism and general hypocrisy were the basic characteristic features of the Zhivkov era.

The second half of the 1960s and the 1970s were the Golden Era of Bulgarian socialism when an extensive economic development led to an increase in incomes and cemented the formula of socialism: meeting demand yet allowing no excess, social security in exchange for complete obedience and opportunity for privileges through legal and semi-legal schemes. Labelled as "the period of stagnation", Leonid Brezhnev's rule in the Soviet Union was for Bulgaria the time when it got the most from the socialist system for the division of labour meant receiving almost free oil and raw materials and getting unlimited access to huge markets with no competition whatsoever.

The condemnation of communism in Bulgaria needs no verbal justification. It is enough to look around and see the ugly and dismal cities, the grey pre-fab dormitory housing in the suburbs, the giant smoke-belching loss-making enterprises, the damage done to the environment, the potholed roads and the deplorable airport of the capital city: traces of occupation with no care for the occupied. People, or "the working people" as they were called, responded with complete alienation. People like millions of ants, some of them enthusiastic and the others sceptical about the results of the Big Experiment. But it was a shared negativism that placed the regime on moving sands. A few dared openly oppose the ruling top-crust. After the killings and emigration of dissidents, opposition and attempts for change were only sporadic. People's patience was exhausted only in the 1980s but there were no signs of political activity: in 1980, Bulgaria with a population of eight million had 817,000 members of the Communist Party. In the early 1980s this artificial model ground to a halt and the insane economic system of mismanagement ran out of momentum. Trying to stay calm, the Communist rulers started taking sizeable loans from Western banks against government security, spending them for keeping up the incomes and the conspicuous lifestyle of the Communist nomenklatura. But the symptoms of a crisis were already observable: some staples were in short supply or missing from stores and there were cyclic crises in fuel and electricity supplies. Talk of modernising the economy, structural reform and new technologies became increasingly frequent and party decisions were taken (1979, 1980) to introduce what was described as a new economic mechanism. Todor Zhivkov and his advisers were trying to introduce what would later be labelled as the Chinese model of state-controlled capitalism. None of these things could be accomplished under the conditions of state monopoly that had already exhausted its economic resources. The time came to pay the bill.

The "perestroika" launched by Mikhail Gorbachev shook the ground under Zhivkov's feet but he managed to hold on to power for several more years till 1989 when impoverishment could no longer be contained, the economy was heading for a collapse and the country was no longer able to repay its huge debts. 1989 saw the most dramatic crisis: the so called "Revival Process" when Bulgarian Turks had their Muslim names forcibly changed to Christian ones and a wave of emigrants moved to Turkey. About 300,000 ethnic Turks left the country for good.This added more fuel to the process of radicalisation of public opinion and 1988–1989 saw the emergence of the first strongholds of opposition: of ethnic Turks and of Bulgarian intellectuals in defense of human rights and in protest against environmental damage. In the wave of revolutions sweeping through the former Soviet bloc, on November 10, 1989, Communist Party functionaries ousted Todor Zhivkov trying to transform themselves into democrats while keeping their comfortable positions. But the collapse of the backbone of the totalitarian system foiled the schemes of the plotters and the country entered a new phase of development.

A new beginning

Since 1989 Bulgaria has been going through a painful transition involving the transformation of the loss-making centralized economy into a market economy; reinstatement of the democratic principles of public life; and promotion of free thinking and guarantees for human liberties. It was for the third time in a century that the whole state has been utterly restructured.

The political transition from a totalitarian system of government toward pluralist democracy proved to be the easiest and most radical change, being at the same time a process of gradual transformation, rather than a revolution. Todor Zhivkov was ousted but still retained his pension and privileges; the attempts to have him sentenced for political crimes over the years proved futile and showed that the real separation from the past would be a long process. In November 1989 the power was delegated to another high communist official, who was expected to continue with gradual reforms and appease public opinion. The end of 1989, however, was the winter of Bulgarians' discontent. The demonstrations with tens of thousands of protesters and the apparent consolidation of the Communist party pushed the scattered opposition groups to form in December 1989 a new political entity – the Union of Democratic Forces (UDF), headed by Zheliu Zhelev, a dissident scholar. The Union came into being as a response to the urgent need of a public voice to represent the anticommunist forces and brought together individuals and entities with disparate interests. This circumstance explains a lot about the subsequent political development in Bulgaria in the following years.

The reshaping of the political system started in January 1990 with the "round table" – the four and a half months long process where the BCP and the UDF, together with a host of other organizations reached agreements that were to shape the future of the country: the agreement to change the constitution immediately and to hold elections under a new electoral law. The UDF against its better judgment agreed to speedy elections and, badly prepared, lost the first pluralist election to the Communist party with 36 to 47 % of the votes. The elections were marked by the appearance of many new small parties, and among others - the newly formed Movement for Rights and Freedoms, the officially registered party of the Bulgarian Turks, which won 4% of the votes and entered Parliament to become a force to be reckoned with. The creation and the existence of the MRF established the Bulgarian ethnic model of political negotiations, which was instrumental in preventing any kind of violent or oppressive actions. The Communist party, already renamed Bulgarian Socialist Party (BSP), formed a government and dominated the Grand National Assembly, elected to adopt a new constitution. A representative of BCP – Petar Mladenov, assumed the newly created position of Chairman (President) of the Republic. His behaviour during the tumultuous months of the Fall of 1990 and the accusation of lying to the people however led to his swift resignation.

The government of Andrej Lukanov was a government of the Socialist party and was faced with the responsibility to start the economic and political reform, expected and demanded by society, being at the same time reluctant to make major changes and trying to preserve its political and economic position. The government declared moratorium on the payment of the country's external debt and for years destroyed its credibility with external creditors and potential investors. Under Lukanov the state fiscal reserve disappeared with no traces and huge amounts of funds were transferred abroad; several companies changed their ownership and were registered abroad. The silent plundering remained hidden from the public and the political forces engaged in bitter debates over the constitution. The scale of the economic ruin became evident by the end of 1990 when virtually everything disappeared from the stores, including bread and milk and for the first time since the war a rationing system was introduced to prevent famine. Lukanov led the country to the brink of catastrophe. The popular unrest and the unwillingness to deal with the chaos, created by his own government, pushed Lukanov to submit his resignation.

The new government was the result of a compromise: it was led by Dimitar Popov, a former judge with no political experience. Having an extremely varied composition, this government of "consensus" lost another year of well-meaning but uncoordinated efforts. In February 1991 the prices of all basic goods were liberalized, actually establishing the premise of the market economy; Bulgaria changed dramatically the priorities of its foreign policy toward the European Union and the United States. On July 12, 1991 the Constituent Assembly, against the objections of the opposition, approved the new Constitution. It introduced and guaranteed the basic principles of the democratic society and formed the groundwork for normal development. Nevertheless, the act proved to be premature and some of the provisions and the imbalances of the Constitution became visible over the years.

After the adoption of the Constitution new elections were scheduled to elect a new Ordinary National Assembly. The UDF entered the election campaign bitterly divided and with changed leadership and won 34.36% of the vote, with the BCP second with 33.14%. The UDF and its new leader Philip Dimitrov formed a government with the support of the MRF (the Turkish party), but without their participation in the government. In the beginning of 1992 Zheliu Zhelev won the first real presidential elections and became President and the democratic face of Bulgaria for the following 5 years. The new government formulated its goal: to change the system and start extensive legislative, economic and diplomatic efforts to put Bulgaria permanently on the democratic track and eliminate the grip of the old communist nomenclature. Bulgaria was accepted in the Council of Europe and in 1992 officially submitted candidature to become a member of the EU. The government policy was facing constant challenge inside and outside of Parliament, attacked even by fellow democrats, such as the President. In a gesture of moral responsibility, the prime-minister submitted a confidence vote and surprisingly the MRF withdrew its support and the government lost the vote.

The next two years, 1993 and 1994, Bulgaria was headed by yet another government of the compromise. Without parliamentary election and using the mandate of the MRF a government was formed, supported for two years by the Socialist Party votes and led by the technocrat-economist Prof. Lyuben Berov. This period became the symbol of the dominance of corporative interests and was marked by behind-the-scene deals, high inflation, non-transparent privatization and the flourishing of the "gray" economic sector. In 1994 the unemployment reached 20.5%. The government of Berov, unable to carry on serious reforms without clear political support, resigned in the autumn of 1994.

The next elections were a sweeping victory for the BSP. The party promoted its new image of a reformist and social-democratic entity led by its young leader Zhan Videnov. It won 43.5% of the vote (in coalition with a few puppet political entities) and formed a government, headed by its leader. The Bulgarian parliament became more diverse (although not much improved in terms of expertise and capacity) with the entry of new political entities. The first year of the socialist rule was time of stabilization and rising GDP, the socialists more or less keeping the orientation toward market economy and openness to Europe. In February 1995 Bulgaria signed the agreement for association with the EU and submitted an official demand for full membership. However, for much of the old communist functionaries this was a time for taking revenge and for availing themselves of the opportunity to be shielded by a "friendly" government. Mismanagement and open robbery led to the worst economic crisis since 1990. The state-owned and "private" banks, run by former officers of the secret services and other shadowy figures used the lack of control to distribute millions of dollars as bad loans and drain the banking system. The banking sector collapsed in a series of bankruptcies, burning the savings of hundreds of thousands of small savers. The huge speculation and lack of control of the grain market provoked bread shortages and chaos. In January 1997 the inflation reached hundreds of percent, the average salary became the equal of a few USD. The presidential election campaign in the fall of 1996 raised sharply the level of political activity. The election of Peter Stoyanov, recognized as the true representative of the UDF as opposing Zheliu Zhelev, regarded by the UDF as a renegade, changed the political situation. Facing huge economic problems and strong internal and external pressure Zhan Videnov resigned, both as prime-minister and as leader of the BSP. The historian Georgi Parvanov became head of the Party.

The Socialist party debated on the possibility to form a new government but under public pressure and facing the mass demonstrations in the streets of Sofia the new leadership returned the mandate to the President, averting worsening of the situation and, coincidentally, pulling out of the dire straits of the ruined economy. At the beginning of 1997 a provisional care-taker government dominated by the UDF was formed to lay the ground for new elections and salvage the collapsing economy. Meanwhile the UDF took course of reinventing itself as a political party and emerged at the elections as a strong centralized party with its new leader the economist Ivan Kostov, already a seasoned politician. The UDF formed a coalition of other right-of-the-center forces and won the impressive absolute majority of 52.26%, which enabled it to form government with strong parliamentary support.

The years of Ivan Kostov's government were the first period of systematic policy toward market reforms, liberalism, establishment of clear rules and Euro-Atlantic integration. The country entered in a currency board, with the full support of the IMF and the national currency remained remarkably stable with a very low inflation rate since. The privatization process changed the structure of Bulgarian economy; the nationalized property and the land were restored to their legitimate owners. Bulgaria started negotiating its accession to the EU and made major steps toward becoming a member of NATO.

The liberal and monetary policy had its high social price. Stability was not accompanied with strong economic growth and the living standards remained very low. The restructuring of the economy and the slow coming of foreign investments maintained a very high unemployment rate, in some places reaching 35 %. The reforming of the welfare system produced major problems with public health care and the pensions remained abysmally low. If we add that some members of the UDF, especially in the provincial towns, took advantage of the period of Kostov's government as an opportunity to get rich, it becomes understandable why popular discontent was on the rise. Publicly voiced accusations of corruption were now addressed openly. The support for the government was dropping sharply.

In 2001 many Bulgarians had already realized that the changes were for good. These included a number of priceless acquisitions in terms of freedoms and liberties, individual autonomy, wide opportunity for economic initiatives, openness to the world, etc. At the same time, it meant that the loss of position, job, status and social privileges was here to last. The last leap of faith that some miracle would replace the painstaking process of building society and the state anew was the coming of the good tsar. In 2001 the exiled former king Simeon Koburg-Gotha came to the country with the promise to improve life and resolve the problems in 800 days if he were given the chance to rule. His ambitions ran in the direction of restoring the monarchy and as a second choice – assuming the Presidency. A ruling of the Constitutional Court closed the way to the presidency and Simeon took the political road, deciding to run in parliamentary elections on a ticket bearing little more than his name and the promise of a "new policy", "honesty", "changing the system" and "end to the partisan bickering". A new political entity was created out of a disparate group of individuals named "National Movement Simeon II" with no platform but a public statement from Simeon.

The disillusionment of the public and the longing for positive messages raised a high tide of expectations. The Movement won 49 % of the vote and formed a government of experts and imported yuppies. The missing one percent of support was provided by the MRF. The Turkish party signed a coalition agreement and for the first time entered the government with two ministers, a few deputy-ministers, a number of regional governors, etc. In the fall of 2001 Peter Stoyanov lost the presidency to Georgi Parvanov, leader of the BSP. His unclear position, the burden of sharing the responsibility with the UDF, the mismanaged campaign and the ambiguous support of Simeon cost him the post.

By the end of 2001 Bulgaria had a former tsar for a Prime Minister and a former communist for a president. At first glance, this situation could be interpreted as a triumph of the nostalgia and a return to the past. The political development after one year of government, however, showed something different and very important: the changes in Bulgaria were irreversible. The government followed more or less the policy of the UDF in the economic and social sphere, which led to a swift disappointment and falling ratings. At present Bulgaria has no other reasonable choice but to continue the market reform. The political process has become that of an established democracy where all the differences are resolved through talks not revolts. The government pursues actively the process of integration in the EU and NATO. And even though the president retains the rhetoric of a "people's" president, he supports more or less consistently the major commitments of Bulgaria.

In 2002 some political scientists in Bulgaria declared the end of the transition. Many others disagreed. And still it is painfully clear to all that social development has no shortcuts and no magic solutions. Bulgarians are facing a long and difficult process of transforming their society into a really modern, democratic society and the cultural transformation will be the longest. A key factor in this transformation will be the acceptance of the fact that individual responsibility and social solidarity are the only foundations on which Bulgarians could build their future.